The
NOTTING HILL &
HOLLAND PARK
BOOK

past and present

First published 2004
by Historical Publications Ltd
32 Ellington Street, London N7 8PL
(Tel: 020 7607 1628)

© Richard Tames 2004
The moral right of the author has been asserted
All rights reserved; unauthorised duplication contravenes applicable laws

ISBN 094667 95 8
British Library Cataloguing-in-Publication Data
A catalogue record for this book is available from the British Library

Production by Liz Morrell and Patrick Donnelly
Printed in Zaragoza, Spain by Edelvives

THE ILLUSTRATIONS

The author and the publisher are grateful to the following for permission to use their illustrations. In some cases it has not been possible to identify or contact the copyright holder so we apologise if any copyrights have been infringed.

Camera Press: *40*
Getty Images: *96*
Guildhall Library, London *47, 49*
Royal Borough of Kensington & Chelsea: *6, 7, 21, 16, 18, 62, 64, 65, 90, 104, 120, 133*
London Metropolitan Archives: *11, 12, 79, 11,*
London Transport Museum: *24*
Museum of London: *68*
National Monuments Record: *115, 121*
National Portrait Gallery: *103, 113*
Richard Tames: *9, 13, 23, 28, 30, 34, 35, 48, 64, 67, 71, 72, 73, 74, 75, 76, 81, 86, 87, 95, 101, 105, 110, 111, 116, 117, 118, 119, 124, 129, 130, 131, 132, 134, 135, 136, 141, 142, 143*
Other illustrations were supplied by the publisher

The
NOTTING HILL AND HOLLAND PARK
BOOK

past and present

Richard Tames

HISTORICAL PUBLICATIONS

Introduction

"The valley ... is laid down with grass and the whole of the district appears to have undergone but little alteration in respect to culture and division of the land for several ages. Although the distance from London is scarcely three miles, yet the traveller may imagine himself to be embosomed in the most sequestered part of the country, and nothing is heard but the notes of the lark, the linnet or the nightingale." Thus, in 1820, Thomas Faulkner could still describe northern Kensington as a rural paradise. Even a generation later, in 1850, Cunningham's *Handbook of London* would describe a far more developed Notting Hill not as a distinctive district in its own right but as "an estate in the parish of Kensington, thickly covered with houses and streets built between the years 1828 and 1848." To this was added an explanation of its etymology ("from the manor of Knotting-bernes") and a pat on the back for "the very handsome modern Gothic church, St. John's". The whole entry ran to eleven lines, slightly more than Numismatic Society, which followed it, and considerably less than Norton Street which preceded it. Holland House, as "the meeeting-place for Whig politicians, for poets, painters, critics and scholars", rated over eighty lines and Kensal Green cemetery almost as many but there was no entry for Holland Park. Or Ladbroke Grove. Or Campden Hill. Or Westbourne Park. Notting Hill and its environs were thus still in a process of becoming established and still pretty much a social wasteland, devoid of celebrity. Indeed, Kensington itself was referred to patronisingly as "almost a part of London".

Between 1820 and 1885 thirteen thousand buildings were put up in what the *Survey of London* defines as 'North Kensington' The vast majority of these were dwellings, but there were also sixteen Anglican churches, fifteen Nonconformist chapels, two Roman Catholic churches and no less than six convents. A trade directory of 1876 lists two and half thousand businesses, pursuing some 220 trades and including 121 publicans.

The peak years of building activity were 1848-53 and 1859-68. Most of the house-building was promoted by speculators, among whom solicitors were especially prominent. Bankruptcies were common and frequently spectacular. Much of the subsequent building that took place between the 1880s and the Great War involved the demolition of large villas to cover their sites and grounds with mansion blocks of apartments. Apart from the erasure of the notorious 'Piggeries' and 'Potteries' of Notting Dale slum clearance was largely deferred to the inter-war period, by which time it was long overdue. In 1923 the infant mortality rate (deaths per thousand live births) in the Golborne area, between today's Westway and Kensal Town, was 107, in Earl's Court 11. In the 1930s Southam Street's 145 houses accommodated 625 families, giving it a resident population of 2,386. A major hollowing out was destined for the following half century. In 1911 the Golborne area had a population of 27,180. By 1991 this had fallen to 7,872.

Wartime bombing necessitated much rebuilding thereafter. In the 1950s North Kensington was at a low ebb, mystifying and alien to former residents like the celebrated cartoonist Osbert Lancaster, who remembered its Edwardian splendour. Notting Hill had become a land of refuges and exiles, of hopeful immigrants and exploitative landlords, decayed stucco and torn curtains, in a word – seedy. A quarter of a century later, in the late 1970s, the locality was redefining itself yet again. Novelist and local resident Emma Tennant noted "a growing number of the middle class ... painting in sorbet colours and thrusting weeping willows into the scruffy ground" and recorded with wonderment the presence of "a famous society beauty who entertains regularly in Elgin Crescent". Of the gustatory delights for which Notting Hill is now known she observed with brutal candour that "the restaurants ... might be of more interest to sociologists than they are to gourmets; they all reflect the different lifestyles of this area with quite remarkable accuracy but few of them are that good to eat at." Leith's, noted as the exception to the dozen listed, was "the sort of place most people can only hope to visit with the aid of a fairy godmother."

And now? Uniquely among London's localities the area now merits its own lifestyle guide, the very excellent *Inside Notting Hill*, compiled by local insiders Miranda Davies and Sarah Anderson and published in the wake of the success of the film *Notting Hill*, which made the locality synonymous with urban chic. The index to *Inside Notting Hill* lists 13 bars and winebars, 29 cafes and takeaways, 22 pubs and 'gastropubs' and 43 'restaurants and bars', not to mention 30 further outlets selling food and wine. Other local preoccupations are revealed by the presence of four florists, five giftshops, six jewellery shops, seven bookshops, eight hairdressers, eight music shops, 17 galleries and 54 fashion and shoe outlets, plus another ten establishments dealing in 'vintage and second-hand clothes'.

An area which in the 1950s was home to Bohemian writers like Colin MacInnes, by the 1970s was attracting future celebrities such as David Hockney, Zandra Rhodes and John Cleese. Twenty years later notable residents would include singers Robbie Williams and Kylie Minogue, designer Stella McCartney, artist Damien Hirst and best-selling author Helen Fielding.

Despite the locality's undeniable image of glamour and affluence, market analysis reveals the continuance of marked social contrasts. The people who live at the top of the hill inhabit what is defined as 'a prosperous enclave of highly qualified executives'. Among them there are few children and a below average proportion of pensioners but a disproportionate number of students and residents in their twenties and thirties. Four-fifths work in service occupations and the proportion with degrees is over four times the national average. *The Guardian* is the most popular newspaper but virtually no one watches ITV. Half of all homes are flat conversions – thirteen times the national average. The proportion of local residents earning over £40,000 per year is double the national norm. Affluence is revealed by high spending on fitness equipment, hardback books, CDs and long holidays in exotic destinations and by the ownership of stocks and shares, although a disproportionate number of households have no car. Those that do have a car have a large, expensive one. Dishwashers are almost universal, microwaves thin on the ground. Eating out is frequent and often Thai or vegetarian. Less than one per cent of the nation's population live in areas like this.

And at the bottom of the hill? The area is characterised by estates with high unemployment of a type almost entirely confined to Inner London. Many residents also live in flats, but these are council flats and purpose-built. There are "severe social problems" associated with high concentrations of the elderly, ethnic minorities and single parent families. Residents here watch ITV a lot, read *The Sun* or *The Mirror* and microwave their meals. Exercise, a healthy diet and home improvement do not figure prominently in their lifestyle; betting, bingo, vodka and heavy smoking do. Half of all residents never take a holiday.

Just over one per cent of the nation's population lives like this. Was it ever thus? Read on.

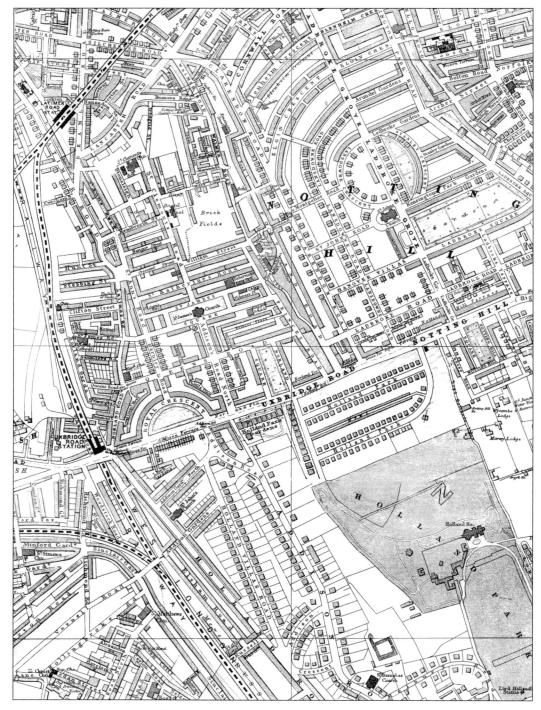

Map of much of the Notting Hill and Holland Park area, c.1888.

The Abbey

The Abbey, a huge Gothic pile of a house, once stood at the corner of Campden Hill Road and Phillimore Walk on a site now occupied by the Central Library. It was built in 1879-80 for a stockbroker called William Abbott – hence The Abbey (his idea of a joke). The architect was Henry Winnock Hayward, who had built the semi-detached Tudor Gothic villas at 6-12 Phillimore Place in 1857. The interior of The Abbey was sumptuously, if not tastefully, decorated with statues and panel paintings celebrating British history. The house was destroyed by bombing in 1941.

Edwin Austin Abbey

Trained in his native Philadelphia, Abbey (1852-1911) was on the staff of prestigious *Harper's Magazine* at 19. Inspired by the paintings of Leighton, Watts and Boughton *(qqv)*, which he saw at the Philadelphia Centennial exhibition in 1876, Abbey journeyed to England in 1878 and emigrated permanently in 1880. In 1885 he went on a sketching holiday with Boughton, by now a close friend, and contributed illustrations to the latter's resulting book.

Abbey was also friendly with Whistler, John Singer Sargent, who sketched his portrait and with Linley Sambourne *(qv)*, with whom he shared a model, Maud Easton, of whom Sambourne took several nude photographs in Abbey's house at 54 Bedford Gardens. Moving on from illustration and water colour, Abbey was elected ARA on the strength of only his second oil painting. Specialising in subjects drawn from history and poetry, in 1902 Abbey was commissioned to produce the official portrayal of Edward VII's coronation, a massive 15' x 9' composition incorporating 120 individual portraits. Abbey also produced large murals for the Royal Exchange, the Boston Public Library and the Pennsylvania state capitol. A man of great charm and learning, Abbey was showered with British, American and French honours and awards.[1]

Joseph Addison

Best remembered as an essayist and for the polished prose of the urbane commentaries on the urban scene that he contributed to the *Tatler* and *The Spectator*, Addison (1672-1719) was a classics don at Magdalen, Oxford, renowned for witty and whimsical Latin verses, before he

1. *Joseph Addison, from a painting by Sir Godfrey Kneller for the Kit-Kat Club.*

entered politics to serve twice as Secretary for Ireland. Addison passed much time holding literary court at Button's coffee-house in Covent Garden, which he had himself initially financed. Marriage to the Countess of Warwick in 1716 regularised Addison's position at Holland House *(qv)* but the alliance proved unhappy, despite his universally acknowledged charm. It had its compensations, however; Addison is said to have composed while strolling the length of his new home's hundred foot library, having placed a glass of wine at either end for refreshment. Addison was buried in Westminster Abbey after calling his stepson to his side to show him with what equanimity a Christian could die.

Dr Johnson in composing his *Life of Addison* praised the balance of his style "on grave subjects not formal, on light occasions not grovelling". Two centuries later the critic Cyril Connolly, conceding Addison to be "the first Man of Letters", excoriated him for having "the misuse of an extensive vocabulary ... the quality of his mind was inferior to the language which he had used to express it." Addison himself hoped that he would be known for having "brought philosophy out of closets and libraries ... to dwell in clubs and assemblies, at tea-tables and coffee-houses."

Addison Road *(qv)*, Addison Grove etc. are named for him, as is a riverside walk at Magdalen College, Oxford.

2. A proposed house in Addison Road, from The Builder 26 May 1883.

Addison Road

Addison Road was laid out with sewers in 1823. The building of semi-detached villas began in 1824. Nos. 40-7 are of 1841-50 and Nos. 36-9 of 1843-5. Charles Richard Fox *(qv)*, had a grand mansion, at No. 1, on the corner of Holland Park Avenue; the house was demolished at his death. Holland Park Lawn Tennis Club occupies part of its grounds, as do Holland Park Court and Carlton Mansions. No. 8 was built by Halsey Ricardo *(qv)*. Oakwood Court is built on the site of a duel in which the extraordinarily quarrelsome 2nd Lord Camelford (1775-1804) was killed by his opponent. Camelford had already managed to get himself sacked from the Royal Navy three times, had got away with shooting dead a fellow officer and had been fined £500 for brawling in a theatre – all by the age of 29. Camelford directed that he should be buried in Switzerland but, war preventing this, his coffin was taken to the crypt of St Anne's, Soho and lost.

Notable residents of Addison Road have included David Lloyd George, John Galsworthy, Radclyffe Hall, Chaim Weizmann *(qv)*, Sir Edward Poynter and Mrs Violet Van der Elst *(qv)*.

William More Adey (1858-1942)

Art critic More Adey was one of the few friends of Oscar Wilde who did not desert him in his disgrace. Indeed he visited him in Reading Gaol and looked after the writer's financial affairs while he was inside. Unfortunately he made such a hash of it that Wilde was furious with him. Adey collaborated with Eric Stenbock *(qv)* in producing a translation of Stenbock's short stories and became co-editor of the *Burlington Magazine*. Adey lived with Wilde's other constant friend Robert Ross (1869-1918) at 24 Hornton Street, then at 15 Vicarage Gardens, between 1905 and 1908. After Ross's death Adey retired to Under-the-Hill House at Wotton-under-Edge in Gloucestershire, which he had inherited and had it entirely demolished in search of a mythical treasure. He died in a mental hospital.

(William) Harrison Ainsworth

Harrison Ainsworth (1805-82) shot to the literary fame he longed for with the publication of *Rookwood* in 1834. He excelled as a story-teller and the book's most famous epi-

3. William Harrison Ainsworth, who lived at Kensal Manor House.

sode, the gripping hundred-page account of Dick Turpin's ride to York, was written in a single stint of twenty-four hours while the author was living at The Elms in Kilburn. Ainsworth confirmed his popularity with vivid descriptions of the plague and fire of London in *Old St Paul's* and by making a folk hero out of Jack Sheppard, a direly incompetent criminal but brilliant escapologist. Further historical romances flowed from his pen; in the end the catalogue of the British Museum would require twenty-three pages to list his publications. Ainsworth prospered further as an editor of monthly magazines. His homes at Kensal Lodge and from March 1841 Kensal Manor House became famed for lavish hospitality. Like Dickens, whom he introduced to the men who would become his close friends – the Count D'Orsay, the novelist Bulwer-Lytton, the painter Daniel Maclise and Dickens' first biographer, John Forster – Ainsworth liked to mark any occasion or achievement he thought significant with a celebratory dinner. Thackeray (who satirised his hosts 'Newgate' novels), and Ainsworth's illustrator, George Cruikshank, were also frequent guests. Ainsworth's Kensal home also became the base for rambles or riding expeditions into what was still the semi-rural fringe of north-west London. Ainsworth's literary popularity declined in the 1850s, forcing him to move to Brighton. He was awarded a Civil List pension in 1856 but was obliged to undertake hack work to survive. Although he died at Reigate, Ainsworth was buried at Kensal Green, a short walk from the former site of his greatest social triumphs.

Alfie

The film that made Michael Caine a household name featured 22 St Stephen's Gardens, Chepstow Road as the apartment occupied by its cynical womanising hero.

All Saints, Talbot Road

The tall, slender tower of All Saints pointed like a reproachful finger to a heavenly vision of what might have been. In 1851 the Reverend Samuel Edward Walker, rector of St Columb Major in Cornwall, the richest living in the county, inherited a large fortune from his father, a Master in Chancery. Between 1852 and 1855 Walker used it to acquire some ninety acres of land in North Kensington, intending to create a new town there with a church and a college of priests at its heart. This he hoped to develop not

4. *William White's design for All Saints church, Talbot Road Work began abortively in 1852, but the building was not entirely finished until 1861.*

only as a model community but as a sufficiently profitable one to enable him to recycle cash to Cornwall to raise his incumbency to the status of a bishopric. Some £66,000 was initially advanced to builders. Work on the church, designed by William White (1825-1900), a pupil of Sir George Gilbert Scott, began in 1852. The collapse of Walker's speculations in 1855 left him with mortgage debts of £90,000 and the church as an undecorated shell, referred to disparagingly as All Sinners in the Mud. Around it stood "a graveyard of buried hopes" – consisting of half-built houses–"naked carcases, crumbling decorations, fractured walls and slimy cement-work". Ladbroke Gardens was nick-named Coffin Row and another row of residences

as The Stumps. All Saints was eventually completed between 1859 and 1861, not by White but by a civil engineer. The originality of White's designs was, however, maintained. The five-stage tower, modelled on that of St Bavo in Ghent, is supported by eye-catching buttresses which terminate in corner pinnacles; both the top two tiers have tall, two-light windows and the topmost tier turns octagonal and is embellished with marble shafts and bands of coloured stone. Coloured tiles and gilding likewise decorate the underside of the eaves. During the 1930s the multi-coloured interior was whitewashed over. Wartime bombing in 1940 and 1944 inflicted severe damage, including the loss of the spire which originally surmounted the tower. Post-war repairs were completed in 1951 and a major cleaning programme was undertaken in the 1980s. The reredos and altar in the south transept were brought from St Columb, Lancaster Road. The chancel painting and stained glass (1955) are by Sir Ninian Comper.

Thomas Allason

Between 1821 and 1823 Allason (1790-1852) was responsible for producing the first draft designs for the development of the Ladbroke estate (*qv*), incorporating the notions of a circus and large communal gardens which were to be realised some thirty years later by his successor, Thomas Allom (*qv*), as a series of concentric crescents. Allason began his professional career as a humble draughtsman in the entourage of John and Edward Spencer Stanhope, visiting the Balkans and Greece in 1814-15, an uncomfortable and hazardous enough enterprise in settled times, even more so in the uncertain period surrounding Napoleon's downfall. Allason returned to the ancient port of Pola in Istria (present day Croatia) in 1816 to make further sketches which resulted in 1819 in the publication by John Murray of Allason's *Picturesque Views of the Antiquities of Pola in Istria*. Allason claimed to be the first person to note the phenomenon of entasis as a feature of Greek architecture. C R Cockerell claimed to have made the same discovery independently at the same time. (Entasis is the subtle curvature of line which enlarges Greek columns to counteract the apparent concavity of columns which are built dead straight; Sir Edwin Lutyens' Cenotaph in Whitehall is a celebrated example of this principle in use.) Allason's volume was dedicated to the Society of Dilettanti, which had plans to erect a building for members on Piccadilly, modelled on the temple of Pola. The gesture, alas, failed to secure Allason admission to the exclusive ranks of that distinguished company and he turned, with what feelings one can only guess, to the more mundane task of designing villas, gardens and crescents, many of which were not to be built until 1841-5. Surviving examples of his work include 12-14 and 23-9 Clarendon Road and 66-8, 80-6 and 109-19 Ladbroke Road. In Linden Gardens (qv) Nos. 38, 38B, 40 and 42 have been attributed to Allason. Ladbroke Square's Grade II listed gardens (qv) were laid out to Allason's designs in 1849. As surveyor of the Pitt estate between Holland Street and Sheffield Terrace Allason also designed the stucco-fronted terraces of 1844 in Holland Walk. His work further afield included repairs on Blenheim Palace and designing the gardens at Alton Towers. Allason's son, also Thomas, was responsible for the interior of the Stock Exchange, built in 1853-4.

George James Allman

Allman (1812-98), an Irishman, renounced medicine to become a botanist and then a pioneer of marine zoology, publishing over a hundred learned papers in this field. A prominent promoter of the British Association for the Advancement of Science and President of the Linnaean Society, Allman lived for some time at 15 Campden Hill Road, from where he corresponded with Charles Darwin (qv). Allman held professorships at Trinity College, Dublin (1844-55) and Edinburgh (1855-70) and was a curator at Harvard (1873).

Thomas Allom

Allom (1804-72) was as celebrated an artist as he was an architect, establishing his reputation with illustrations for books on picturesque English counties, such as Cumberland, Westmorland, Devon and Cornwall, on popular British tourist destinations such as France, Belgium, Switzerland and Scotland, and on exotic locations such as Constantinople, Asia Minor and China. These were substantial works, their subject-matter covering architecture, social customs and lifestyles. *Constantinople and the Scenery of the Seven Churches of Asia Minor,* published in 1838 in two volumes, had a text by Robert Walsh, the local British embassy's chaplain. The book was subsequently republished in French and supplies the source matter for a modern appreciation *Thomas Allom's Istanbul* by Turgay Tuna (2000). (At the time of writing a copy of the original Walsh book would cost £300.) Allom's China volume was published in 1843 to take advantage of the heightened public interest created by Britain's acquisition of Hong Kong the previous year. It contained 120 pictures which range over the highlights of the recent fighting and the tea, silk and rice industries as well as the expected pagodas, junks and joss-houses. Abundant detail did not necessarily imply strict accuracy. Allom's landscapes were often over-dramatised to exploit their 'Romantic' potential. Celebrated as a topographical artist, Allom was also in demand within the architectural profession and collaborated frequently with Sir Charles Barry, architect of the Houses of Parliament. Indeed, Allom's first exhibited work, at the Royal Academy in 1824, was a design for a cathedral.

In 1844 Barry commissioned Allom to produce watercolours of his 'New Palace of Westminster' as it would look when completed. These were presented to Tsar Nicholas I on the occasion of his visit to the project in the course of its construction. In 1990, on the occasion of President Gorbachev's visit to the UK, he and Mrs Thatcher autographed twenty-five copies of prints of Allom's views to be sold for charity.

Allom's career as an artist thus complemented his work as an architect. He had served a thorough seven-year apprenticeship in the offices of Francis Goodwin, studied at the Royal Academy Schools and was a founder member of the Royal Institute of British Architects.

Surviving buildings on the Ladbroke estate for which Allom was directly responsible include most of Stanley Gardens, 10-11 Stanley Crescent, 36-40 and 60-8 Ladbroke Grove, 1-3 Ladbroke Gardens, 24 Kensington Park Gardens (1853) and St Peter, Kensington Park Road (1852) *(qv)*. His other projects included workhouses at Marloes Road, Kensington, at Calne in Wiltshire and in Liverpool, a funerary chapel and interiors at Highclere, Hants. for the Earls of Carnarvon, Kensington Cemetery at Ealing, Christchurch, Highbury and Holy Trinity, Barnes, where he died. Allom may be a minor figure in his native land but, to judge by the evidence of contemporary websites, as an artist he is still praised from Turkey to China.[2]

5. *Lady-in-waiting – Queen Anne, a tenant at Campden House before her accession to the throne.*

Queen Anne

From 1691 to 1696 Anne (1665-1714), then Princess of Denmark, rented Campden House. Queen Mary, Anne's sister, until her death in 1694 reigned jointly with her husband, the Dutch Stadholder, William III and had acquired Sheffield House, which they remodelled to become Kensington Palace.

Anne heartily disliked her royal brother-in-law and therefore maintained her own separate household, accessible to, but separate from, the new palace. William had repeatedly snubbed Anne's adored (if admittedly very stupid) husband, George of Denmark, denying him the military employment for which he yearned. William also suspected Marlborough, the ambitious husband of Anne's favourite, Sarah Churchill, of treasonous intrigues with his own exiled father-in-law, the deposed James II.

Mary's death from small-pox in Kensington Palace began the process of reconciliation between Anne and the childless William, who, accepting her position as his nominated successor, deemed it prudent to behave more civilly towards her lest she become a focus of further intrigues. In 1696 he therefore put St James's Palace at Anne's disposal and she vacated her Campden Hill eyrie. Anne and her husband later subscribed £80 towards the costs of Kensington's parish school.

James Archer

In 1862 Archer (1823-1904) abandoned the large portraiture practice he had built up in Edinburgh to settle at 21 Phillimore Gardens, moving to 7 Cromwell Place in 1882. His forte became historical costume pictures (*The Death of King Arthur*) and portraits of children, being the first artist to paint them in period costume. At the time of writing his 'A woman in a red Sari standing in a doorway', dated 1888, was offered for sale at £20,000.

Artesian Well

What is alleged to have been England's first artesian well was sunk in 1794 in the grounds of the home of Benjamin Vulliamy *(qv)*, later occupied by No. 130 Holland Park Avenue. A four foot shaft 236 feet deep was sunk and a further 25 feet boring of 5.5 inches was made to yield a flow of 45 gallons a minute. The water was said to be especially good for washing. The well was covered over in 1840.

6. *The nursery at Aubrey House, 1817. From a watercolour by Mrs L Goldsmid.*

Aubrey House

The house is named after Aubrey de Vere, companion of William the Conqueror and first lord of the manor of Kensington. It was originally called Wells House because its construction in 1698 was prompted by the discovery of mineral waters on Campden Hill. The main backers of the scheme to promote this as a spa were a 'doctor of Physick', John Wright, and apothecary John Stone. The venue was endorsed in 1699 by Dr Benjamin Allen's survey of the *Natural History of the Chalybeat and Purging Waters of England*. In 1705 J Bowack's *Antiquities of Middlesex* referred to it as "a famous Chalybial Spring much esteemed and resorted to for its Medicinal Virtues" but Wells House's incarnation as a spa was brief-lived, although John Rocque's map of 1746 still marks Kensington Wells to the north-east of Holland House. By the 1720s the building was referred to as a 'Villa at Nottin (sic) Hill', then called Notting Hill House, in the possession of Edward, later Sir Edward, Lloyd, Secretary of War, who added wings to the building. As Aubrey House, it was let by Lloyd, from 1767 to 1788, to Lady Mary Coke (1726-1811), a widow whose albino complexion and taste for gossip gained her the nickname of 'the White Cat'. Lady Mary was wealthy enough to have her portrait painted in 1762 by the Scottish master Allan Ramsay, then in peak demand, having just painted the official coronation portrait of

7. In musical mode – Lady Mary Coke, from a painting by Allan Ramsay, 1762.

the new king, George III. She could also afford to employ the fashionable architect James Wyatt to decorate her drawing room. Lady Mary indulged a passion for gardening in extensive grounds which extended over what are now Aubrey Road (then an avenue of lime trees) and Campden Hill Square (qv) and yielded plentiful crops of plums, pears and apples which were on occasion comprehensively plundered by night to her great annoyance. The situation and outlook of the house was still sufficiently rural for her to keep cows and, when one wandered off in the direction of London, she joked that it was obviously bored by the countryside. On the other hand she was very put out in 1774 when a hunt in full cry crashed through her grounds, as such an intrusion "so near London was not to be expected". Passing traffic was, however, sufficient for her to have an artificial mound thrown up so that she could watch the world go by, possibly in imitation of the one erected by the late Queen Caroline in Kensington Gardens. Lady Mary's other preoccupations were letter-writing and her journal. In October 1772 she recorded that while reading in her library in the evening she heard a pistol shot, which turned out to be the shooting of a highwayman on the road outside her grounds. Extensive extracts from her letters and journals were edited and published in 1889-96 by the Hon. J A Home. In the 1820s the house was in the possession of Joshua Flesher Hanson

developer of Campden Hill Square (qv). From 1830 to 1854 it accommodated a private boarding school for young ladies, one of many in the locality but probably one of the better ones. In 1859 occupancy passed to Peter Alfred Taylor (1819-91) who finally achieved his ambition to enter the Commons at the third attempt in 1862, as MP for Leicester. Taylor was a radical champion of the progressive causes of the day, ranging from Italian unification (Mazzini, who lived in Brompton, was a personal friend) to working class education and international arbitration. In 1865 Taylor entertained Louisa May Alcott (author of *Little Women*) for ten days at the request of Ralph Waldo Emerson. Taylor invited round Gladstone, Mazzini and Dickens and took her to Parliament to hear Disraeli and John Stuart Mill debate the merits of the Second Reform Bill. A warm supporter of the Abolitionist movement Taylor had already given his hospitality to the American ex-slave and abolitionist campaigner Frederick Douglass. In 1873 Aubrey House passed into the hands of the Alexander family for the next century. William Cleverley Alexander, a banker, (1840-1916) was both a local philanthropist, a local artist and a local patron of the arts. Early to recognise the talents of James Whistler, he commissioned the artist to paint a portrait of his nine year old daughter, Cicely. The result was one of Whistler's greatest triumphs, *An Arrangement

in Grey and Green*, reckoned among the treasures of the National Gallery, to which it was bequeathed. The sitter (actually stander) might have taken a more jaundiced view as the perfectionist Whistler required no less than seventy sittings over the years 1872-6 and frequently reduced his bored and frustrated subject to tears. Despite this Whistler also painted portraits of two of her sisters, May and Grace, and worked on decorative schemes for Aubrey House.

Alexander himself produced a number of views of the surrounding locality and hosted meetings of the Pen and Pencil club. Aubrey House remained in the possession of the Alexander family until the death of the last of W C Alexander's daughters in 1972. A history of the property was written by local historian Florence M Gladstone in 1922.

Aubrey Lodge was for many years the home of Baroness (Mary) Stocks (1891-1975). Born at Queen's Gate, Kensington she was a granddaughter of Sir William Rendel (qv). Her academic career culminated in becoming principal of Westfield College (1939-51) after which she became nationally known as an outspoken broadcaster, strongly opinionated in the best sense of the word and able to speak with expertise on a wide range of social issues, thanks to her extensive experience as a magistrate and involvement in university settlement work. An economist by training, she wrote histories of the WEA and district nursing and biographies of Eleanor Rathbone and Ernest Simon.[3]

Wycombe Lodge was built on the former kitchen garden of Aubrey House in 1829 and occupied by the Dowager Marchioness of Lansdowne. It was knocked down in 1868 to make way for the Water Works reservoir.

Baptist Chapel, Westbourne Grove

Built to the designs of C G Searle and opened in 1853, it was extended in 1866 to accommodate up to 2,000 worshippers. In 2001-4 the building was restructured within its original façade for church and community use, with apartments above.[4]

Mary Bayley

"The cornerstone of the commonwealth is the hearthstone" wrote Mary Bayley (1816?-94), a resident of Lansdowne Crescent, who took the lead in tackling conditions in the Potteries (qv), forming a Mothers' Society in 1853; a decade later there were four such groups. In 1859 she published *Ragged Homes and How to Mend Them*. The book became sufficiently well known to be recommended by Bishop Bedell in his handbook on pastoral work as the sort of title young women should be advised to read after confirmation as they sought to apply Christian principles to their everyday lives. It was also published in an American Sunday School Union edition in 1864. In 1861 Captain and Mary Bayley opened a Work-

man's Hall in Portland Road as the focal point of a temperance crusade. The Workman's Hall was closed in 1866. Her effort to develop free Turkish baths (qv) proved abortive.

Bedford Gardens

No. 4 was home to composer Frank Bridge (qv), No. 6 to genre painter Edward Sherard Kennedy (died 1910), No. 52 to journalist H E Watts, No. 54 to American painter Edwin Austin Abbey (qv), No. 67 to the Scottish naturalist Andrew Murray and No. 77 to 'The Roberts', Colquhon and MacBryde (qv). Marie Rambert (qv) ran her first (1920-27) ballet school in Bedford Gardens. Impresario Charles Hayden Coffin (1862-1935) also lived in Bedford Gardens.

Bedford Lodge

Built by John Tasker this house was first occupied (1815-19) by (the future General Sir) John Fraser, who later returned to the area to occupy Niddry Lodge (qv). It was the home of the Duke and Duchess of Bedford from 1823 onwards. The Duke employed Sir Jeffrey Wyattville, Gothiciser of Windsor Castle, to extend the house. The Duchess had the drawing-room decorated with white and gold panelling from a French chateau and had painter Sir Edwin Landseer advise her on the layout of her gardens. As Dowager the Duchess remained in occupation until her death in 1853. Bedford Lodge was then taken by the

Duke and Duchess of Argyll and re-named Argyll Lodge. The family, numbering eight, was waited on by twenty-seven servants. The Duchess was instrumental in persuading the historian Macaulay (qv) to take nearby Holly Lodge. The eighth Duke of Argyll (1823-1900) had a long and active political career, paralleled by one as an amateur scientist, though in the latter capacity he was more notable for his taste for controversy than for his scholarship. Created FRS at twenty-eight, in the same year he became chancellor of St Andrew's and in 1854 rector of Glasgow, despite never having been to any university himself. The Duke's occupation of Bedford Lodge was occasioned by the need for a London home when invited to join the government of Lord Aberdeen, though not yet thirty. A powerful parliamentary orator, he consistently supported progressive causes and exerted an important influence on British policy in Ireland and India. His first duchess was doubtless fully occupied in giving him twelve children. The Duke's other major recreation was bird-watching, preferably in his native west of Scotland but otherwise in the grounds of Bedford Lodge. Watts (qv) painted the Duke's portrait. After the Duke's death Bedford Lodge became the home of the ground landlord, who renamed it Cam House, after a Phillimore property in Gloucestershire. Sir Walter Phillimore (1845-1929), son and grandson of eminent lawyers, became an outstanding expert on ecclesiastical and admiralty law, a judge noted for both swiftness and severity and an international jurist of European standing. He served as mayor of Kensington from 1909 to 1911. After his death the house was leased to the wealthy Mrs St George who indulged a characteristically American taste for extravagant interior decor by employing an army of three hundred craftsmen to transform the house and build another dwelling, Plane Tree House, in the garden. Among her whimsical touches were the installation of new entrance gates surmounted by fish-shaped lanterns and the insertion in a garden wall of a door saved from the demolition of Newgate Prison (or doubtless so she was told). On the frontage of the villa, punning on her own name, she had the figures of St George and the Dragon erected. Both houses were taken over by the Army during World War Two and demolished in 1955 to make way for Holland Park School (qv).

The Beatles

Scenes for *A Hard Day's Night* (1964) were shot in Notting Hill, most notably the 'police station' at 83 Clarendon Road, formerly St John's Secondary School.

Tony Benn (1925 -)

A long-term (fifty years) resident of Holland Park Avenue, Benn, the son, grandson and father of MPs, became the longest serving Labour MP in the history of the party and a national figure as a Cabinet minister in Harold Wilson's governments. He retired after fifty years in Parliament "to devote more time to politics". Benn's highly successful one man show *An Audience with Tony Benn* demonstrated that he was held in great affection by the public, most of whom did not share his political views. His eight volumes of political diaries alone (culled from 18,000,000 recorded words) would assure his place in public memory. Benn's wife, Caroline (1926-2000), was the nation's most prominent advocate of comprehensive education and for 35 years a governor of Holland Park School (qv).[5]

Books for Cooks

Founded in 1983 by Heidi Lascelles, who had been a nurse rather than a professional cook or bookseller, Books for Cooks initially opened on the opposite side of Blenheim Crescent from where it now stands. Moving to larger premises at No. 4 made it possible to open the test kitchen where cook Annie Bell could try out recipes. Celebrity cook and TV presenter Clarissa Dickson Wright managed the shop for three years. Since 1994 Rosie Kindersley has been in charge. Resident French chef Eric Treuille runs the workshop programme in collaboration with a team of specialists drawing on expertise in Italian, Japanese, American and vegetarian cuisines. Books for Cooks began publishing its own cookbooks in 1995. The shop's stock runs to over 8,000 volumes from recipe books and works on nutrition to food-related publications in such fields as art, biography, history, sociology and fiction. Having retired to Tuscany, Heidi Lascelles now runs culinary holidays there in association with the bookshop.

Blenheim Crescent is also home to Garden Books at No. 11, Britain's only specialist gardening bookshop and The Travel Bookshop at No. 13 (qv).[6]

George Henry Boughton

Norfolk-born but raised in Albany, New York State, the largely self-taught Boughton (1833-1905) studied in Paris in 1860-1, where he made friends with Whistler. Like many other artists in rapidly industrialising Britain Boughton sought inspiration in the surviving quaintness of such accessible but still strongly rural and culturally distinctive areas as Brittany and the Netherlands. He came to specialise in two highly rewarding genres – peaceful scenes of European peasant life ("nice girls standing around doing not much" in the words of one critic) and of a romanticised New England in Puritan days, which naturally sold well in America. He also illustrated editions of the New England tales of Washington Irving and Nathaniel Hawthorne. Boughton could write as well as paint and contributed short stories to *Harper's Magazine* and the *Pall Mall Magazine*. His *Sketching Rambles in Holland* (1885) combined his own illustrations with those of his

8. *West House in Campden Hill, c.1878, built for George Boughton. The architect was Richard Norman Shaw.*

9. *Frank Bridge's home at 4 Bedford Gardens.*

fellow traveller, Edwin Austin Abbey *(qv)*. Boughton, who exhibited annually at the Royal Academy from 1863 until his death, was wealthy enough to have a residence, West House, at the corner of Campden Hill Road and Peel Street, built for him in 1876 to the designs of his friend, Richard Norman Shaw *(qv)*, who included one of his standard trademarks in the shape of a soaring chimneystack. It was here that Boughton eventually died. The fashionable society portraitist Philip de Laszlo (1869-1937) *(qv)* later had a studio in West House.

(Angelo) Robert Brandard (1805-62)

A painter in both oils and water-colours, Brandard became best known for engravings of the works of Turner and of contemporaries, such as Callcott *(qv)*. He died at his residence, 2 Campden Hill

Villas. Brandard''s brother, Edward (1819-98) engraved the illustrations in Allom's *(qv)* best-selling book on China.

Bill Brandt (1904-83)

After working in Man Ray's Paris studio Brandt established his photographic reputation in the 1930s with studies of urban contrasts – *The English at Home* (1936), *A Night in London* (1938) – and worked for the Ministry of Information during the Blitz. In the late 1940s and 1950s, however, the 'poet of darkness' used an ancient, shutterless wooden Kodak to accumulate a series of abstract nude studies which verged on the Surreal and were published as *Perspective of Nudes* (1961) and *Shadows of Light* (1966).

Many photographs are recorded as having been taken in Campden Hill, although Brandt lived in Belsize Park.[7]

Frank Bridge

A pupil of Stanford *(qv)*, Bridge (1879-1941) was a viola player and conductor and teacher of Benjamin Britten *(qv)*, whose *Variations on a Theme of Frank Bridge* (1937) are based on Bridge's *Idyll No. 2* for string quartet. Bridge, who lived at 4 Bedford Gardens from 1914 onwards, remained a lifelong musical influence on Britten.[8]

Hablot Browne (1815-82)

Hablot Knight Browne (1815-82)–*a.k.a.* 'Phiz'–is best known for his many illustrations of the works of Charles Dickens but he also illustrated for Harrison Ainsworth *(qv)*, notably his *Old St Paul's*. Browne had ambitions to paint in oils but lacked a formal training. He was, however, very good at drawing horses, a reflection perhaps of his own passion for riding to hounds. Stricken by paralysis in 1867, he was able to work but little thereafter and hunt not at all. Browne

10. *Hablot K. Browne ('Phiz') in later life.*

11. *Tower House at 29 Melbury Road, built by William Burges. Below (12) is his bedroom.*

lived at 99 Ladbroke Grove from 1872 to 1880, when he retired to Brighton. His unusual given name was in memory of his sister Katherine's fiancé, an officer of Napoleon's Imperial Guard who fell at Waterloo.

William Burges
In a street of imposing residences none is more striking than No. 29 (until 1967 No. 9) Melbury Road (*qv*), 'Tower House' built by William Burges (1827-81) for himself in 1876-8. The fantastically decorated interior consisted of themed rooms – a hall devoted to Time, drawing-room to Love and library to the Liberal Arts etc. Burges' own deep red bedroom featured convex ceiling mirrors to diffuse candlelight, plus a gold and silver mermaid chimneypiece. He also had an entire room given over to his collection of armour. The son of an engineer, Burges himself studied engineering at King's College, London but

enrolled in the architectural offices of Edward Blore and Matthew Digby Wyatt and then undertook a lengthy continental pilgrimage in search of the Gothic. His reward was a series of prestigious commissions – the

decoration of the chapter house of Salisbury cathedral, cathedrals for Brisbane and Cork, a college at Hartford, Connecticut, a grammar school at Ripon, restoration work at Waltham Abbey and the virtual reconstruction of

13. *A tomb designed by William Burges in Kensal Green Cemetery for Captain C S R Ricketts (1788-1867).*

Cardiff Castle and Castel Coch nearby for the Marquess of Bute *(qv)*. The myopic Burges, a fan of ratting and opium, was also a prolific designer of furniture and jewellery and a discerning collector of Japanese prints, illuminated manuscripts and medieval armour. He only lived at Tower House for three years. Satanist Aleister Crowley (1875-1947) ("the wickedest man in the world") was a subsequent occupant. From 1962 to 1966 the building was empty and suffered vandalism. In 1969 the Irish film actor Richard Harris undertook a complete restoration before selling the house on to Led Zeppelin's Jimmy Page in 1974. Page composed the music for *Death Wish II* for his neighbour Michael Winner, occupant of the former home of Sir Luke Fildes *(qv)*. Examples of William Burges' furniture can be seen in the British Galleries of the British Museum. In Kensal Green cemetery there is a particularly splendid tomb of granite and artificial

stone which Burges designed for Captain C S R Ricketts *(see above)*. Four hundred of the working drawings which Burges made for the interior decoration of Tower House are preserved at the Royal Institute of British Architects.[9]

Bute House

Bute House was possibly the earliest of the Campden Hill villas built by John Tasker. Its first resident, in 1812, was Richard Gillow, probably of the cabinet-making firm of

Waring & Gillow, and a member of a prominent Catholic family. The house took its name from John Crichton-Stuart, second Marquess of Bute (1793-1848), who occupied it from 1830 to 1842. He owned 100,000 acres, most of it in Scotland, but also including the site of Dowlais in South Wales, the world's largest ironworks. By building docks at Cardiff and opening up the Rhondda coalfield Bute virtually created industrial Wales single-handed. Plagued by eye-troubles the Marquess led a reclusive private life but dutifully undertook public duties in local government and the militia. The son born to him a year before his death grew up to receive the largest mineral royalties in Britain and used his fortune to commission William Burges *(qv)* to restore Cardiff Castle. Later occupants of Bute House included the Hon. William Sebright Lascelles MP (1842-51) and Charles Manners, the sixth Duke of Rutland (1865-88). Bute House was demolished in

14. *Bute House in Campden Hill.*

1913. In 1914 the University of London took a 999-year lease on the site for what became Queen Elizabeth College *(qv)*.

Byam Shaw School of Drawing and Painting

This Campden Street establishment was opened in 1911 by John Byam Lister Shaw (1872-1919) and Reginald Rex Vicat Cole (1870-1940), son of George Vicat Cole *(qv)*. Shaw, once characterised as "a kind of belated Pre-Raphaelite", had trained at the St John's Wood School of Art and the Royal Academy. His painterly output consisted of pictures with titles like *Whither?* and *Love's Baubles* but he was also elected an associate of the Royal Society of Painters in Water Colours in 1913. A Byam Shaw window, depicting SS Cecilia and Margaret, can be seen in St Barnabas' church *(qv)*, where there is also his monument – "a recumbent effigy with a startling figure of the risen Christ." Shaw was more productive as an illustrator of literary classics such as Browning, Boccaccio, Poe and Shakespeare, though he was not above *Comic Cuts*.

Eleanor Fortescue Brickdale (1872-1945), another fecund book illustrator, also taught at the school. Graduates included Evie Hone and Winifred Nicholson (née Roberts) artist wife of Ben Nicholson, a nephew of James Pryde *(qv)*. The school moved to Archway in the 1980s and merged with Central St Martin's to become part of the London Institute in 2003.[10]

15. Sir Augustus Wall Callcott, from a portrait by Sir Edwin Landseer.

Sir Augustus Wall Callcott

Born in "the Mall, Kensington Gravel Pits", a terrace on the site now occupied by the Essex Unitarian church, Callcott (1779-1844) was a Westminster Abbey choir boy before training as a painter under Hoppner and specialising in coastal and maritime scenes. His wife, Maria (1785-1842), was a successful author of children's books and creator of the character Little Arthur. Callcott, knighted by Victoria in 1837, became Surveyor of the Queen's Pictures and died in the house in which he had been born. He was buried at Kensal Green cemetery *(qv)*.

John Wall Callcott

The son of a Kensington builder, Callcott (1766-1821) became a prolific composer of glees, organist of St Paul's, Covent Garden and bandmaster of the Kensington Volunteers, of which he was an officer until his career effectively ended in 1807 with the onset of mental illness. His son William Hutchins Callcott (1807-82), born that same year, produced hundreds of arrangements for the piano in an unspectacular career dogged by ill-health and terminated at his residence 1 Campden House Road. His son-in-law was the musician William Horsley (1774-1858), who was also famed for glees.

Campden Charities, 27a Pembridge Villas

Founded in 1629 by Baptist Hicks *(qv)*, Viscount Campden, for the benefit of residents of Kensington, this charitable bequest was intended to relieve poverty among the old and to support education and vocational training.

Organised in its current form in 1990, the charity confines its grants to residents living north of the Fulham Road. From the revenues arising from assets of over £60,000,000 in 2002-3 the Charities made 661 grants totalling £635,559 to individuals, paid £220,125 to 422 pensioners and 53 grants totalling £585,008 to organisations concerned with Moroccan women, travellers, bereavement care, pre-school learning, dance education, video-making etc.

A further £86,000 was granted towards holidays, playschemes and Christmas activities and £230,000 in one-off grants ranging from IT equipment for local primary schools to a vehicle for the local Air Training Corps and musical equipment for Holland Park School.[11]

Campden Grove

Chemist and mountaineer John Norman Collie (1859-1942) lived at No. 16; during six expeditions to the Canadian Rockies between 1897 and 1911 he made 21 first ascents and named at least 30 peaks. Poet Roy Campbell (1901-57) lived at No. 17 in the 1950s. During this period he published a major study of the Spanish poet Garcia Lorca, having himself fought in the Spanish civil war (for Franco). Artist Aubrey Beardsley (1872-98), exhausted by his contributions to *The Yellow Book* and desperately ill with TB, rested at No. 19 in 1896, forbidden to work. James Joyce (1882-1941) lived at 28B in 1931; aged 39 he was preoccupied with regularizing his marriage and disliked the area, which he referred to as 'Campden Grave'.

Campden Hill

Charles Dickens Jnr's *Dictionary of London* (1879) noted that "in point of health the top of Campden Hill is one of the choicest situations in London." In Graham Greene's *Ministry of Fear* (1943) Mrs Bellair's house is described as "old and unrenovated standing among the To Let boards on the slope of Campden Hill." Campden Hill residents have included artists Thomas Faed, Robert Brandard, Anna Maria Charretie, Alfred Rankley, T C L Rowbotham and Sir William Llewellyn, sculptor William Theed, musician Sir George Henschel, connoisseur W G Rawlinson (*qqv*) and anthropologist J F McLennan.

16. *5 Campden Hill Square in 1947.*

Campden Hill Road

It is claimed that London's first mosque was at 111 Campden Hill Road, perhaps as early as 1886; it appears to have remained in existence until the 1930s.

Sir Henry Newbolt (1862-1938), who lived at No. 29 from 1918 until his death, is chiefly remembered for rousing patriotic verses such as *Drake's Drum*, which long enjoyed favour in school anthologies. He also wrote a naval history of the Great War. Ford Madox Ford (*qv*) lived at No. 80. The future Poet Laureate (1968) Cecil Day-Lewis (1904-72), then Professor of Poetry at Oxford, lived at No. 96 from 1953 to 1958, where his son, the actor Daniel Day-Lewis was born in 1957. Dunhill's tobacco and pipe business was also on this road.

Campden Hill Square

Originally known by the name of its first developer Joshua Flesher Hanson (1782-

1847) it soon became Notting Hill Square and in 1893 changed its name to Campden Hill Square to dissociate itself from Notting Hill. Hanson was not only involved in developing Peel Street and the Ladbroke estate as well but was also the major promoter of Regency Square, Brighton, on which his Campden Hill venture was based.

Hanson himself lived at No. 2 (1828-30). J M W Turner came to the garden regularly to paint sunsets. Since 1832 the five hectare garden has beeen managed by a residents' committee which Hanson set up.

Spymaster Roger Hollis lived at No. 6. No. 9 was the home of explorer John McDouall Stuart and No. 11 of cartoonist Phil May *(qqv)*.

No. 13 was the home of Trotskyite Morgan Delt (David Warner) and his posh wife Leonie (Vanessa Redgrave) in the 1966 cult movie *Morgan – A Suitable Case for Treatment*. No. 16 was the home of critic Charles Morgan *(qv)*.

Siegfried Sassoon *(qv)* lived at No. 23 (1925-32). In the 1890s this had been the home of the Llewellyn Davies family, the inspiration for the Darling family in J M Barrie's *Peter Pan* (1904). When the children were orphaned in 1910 Barrie became their guardian. Other literary inhabitants have included Evelyn Underhill *(qv)*, crime writer P D James and dramatist Harold Pinter and biographer Lady Antonia Fraser.

The suffragette refuge at No. 2, owned by a Mrs Brackenbury and known as 'Mouse Castle', got its name from the notorious Prisoner's Temporary Discharge of Ill-Health Act of 1913, more familiarly known as the 'Cat and Mouse Act', which empowered the authorities to release suffragettes on hunger-strike and then re-arrest them when they had recovered sufficiently to serve out more of their sentences. Suffragettes subjected to this treatment were referred to as 'mice' and sent to Mouse Castle to restore their health. The local suffragette HQ was in a shop on the corner of Edge Street and known as Painted Corner from being decorated in the virulent colour scheme of the movement – purple, white and green.

17. *Campden House in 1647, then the residence of Viscount Campden.*

18. *Campden House c.1860, south-east view from the garden. Coloured itho by Edwin Smith.*

19. *Wilson Carlile, founder of the Church Army.*

Campden House

Built in 1612 by Baptist Hicks *(qv)* on lands allegedly acquired, at least in part, in settlement of a gaming debt by Sir Walter Cope *(qv)*, this imposing mansion stood in grounds now bounded by Sheffield Terrace, Hornton Street, Gloucester Walk and Kensington Church Street. The house may not have been entirely new but an enlargement and refacing in stone and brick of a timber residence inhabited by Cope in the 1590s. During the civil wars the house was used by the Committee of Sequestrations for Middlesex, which stripped royalist loyalists of their estates.

Queen Anne *(qv)* leased Campden House in the 1690s. It then became the childhood home of Richard Boyle, third Earl of Burlington (1695-1753), art connoisseur, pioneer of the Grand Tour and promoter of Palladianism. After him came the clever but quarrelsome Attorney-General Nicholas, first Lord Lechmere (1675-1727), who died of apoplexy at his own dining-table.

In 1751 Campden House was sold off for use as a girls' boarding school. By 1795 the building had been updated by the removal of its parapets and other Jacobean ornamentation and the whole stuccoed over. It returned to private occupation in 1847. Its occupant W F Wolley installed a theatre where Dickens *(qv)* acted in 1854. Burned down in 1862, it was lavishly rebuilt in facsimile, only to be demolished in 1900 to make way for Campden House Court.

Prebendary Wilson Carlile

Carlile (1847-1942) became curate of St Mary Abbot's in 1880 but resigned holy orders two years later to found the Church Army. He lived at 34 Sheffield Terrace from 1881 to 1891.[12]

Carmelite Church, Kensington Church Street

The original Carmelite community established on this site, the first in England, was founded by Father Herman (Cohen), a German Jewish convert and musician, in 1862. The first church, designed by Edward Welby

20. *The south doorway of the Carmelite priory in Duke's Lane.*

Pugin, opened in 1866 and was destroyed by bombing in 1940. The church organ, made by the eminent French organ-builder Cavaille-Coll, was first played by the composer Widor. The present Church and Priory of Our Lady of Mount Carmel and St Simon Stock was built in 1955-9 as one of the last works of Sir Giles Gilbert Scott (1880-1960), designer of the red telephone box and grandson of the architect of St Mary Abbots *(qv)*. It is said (not implausibly) to be built on the garden of Sir Isaac Newton's *(qv)* last home.

Carnival

Notting Hill's annual carnival, held over the last weekend in August, is the largest human assemblage in Europe, surpassed on a global scale only by the Muslim pilgrimage to Mecca and, as a street party, itself surpassing the legendary carnival of Rio de Janeiro. Yet forty years ago it did not exist. The social needs it meets and the cultural currents it expresses have therefore become of profound interest to scholars. Over time it has evolved from novelty to curiosity to confrontation to phenomenon to institution. Carnival originated in the aftermath of the 1958 Notting Hill 'riots' *(qv)*. Its first moving spirit, Trinidadian-born Claudia Jones *(qv)*, editor of the Brixton-based and newly-founded *West Indian Gazette*, determined to promote a positive response to the profoundly dispiriting events of the summer of 1958. The pro-

totype, timed to coincide with its Trinidadian inspiration, was held in St Pancras Town Hall on 30th January 1959 and televised on BBC as a pop music event. Carnival continued as an indoor phenomenon until Claudia Jones' death in 1964. In 1965 Rhaune Laslett (died 2002) organised a week-long programme, intended to involve not only Afro-Caribbean peoples but also Irish, Iberians, Ukrainians and other communities in Notting Hill, to culminate in a parade on August Bank Holiday, which police estimated to have attracted a thousand people. Laslett was a play group organiser and the initial emphasis was on children having fun by dressing up. A Carnival Development Committee was formed in 1972. Jamaican-style sound systems were introduced in 1975. As numbers swelled the event began to attract the concern of a variety of constituencies, from Black Power groups to the police. Because carnival is by definition both orchestrated and spontaneous, massive but individualistic, assertive but subversive, its 'ownership' became problematic and contested, with the organising body often riven by rivalries and having to reinvent itself. The police in response were constantly obliged to review their posture and procedures. By 1975 the police estimated attendance at 150,000. In 1976 there was a level of violence – 500 injured – which inspired Mick Jones of The Clash to write *White Riot*. The police response was saturation – the 1,500 police deployed in 1976

became 13,000 by 1981. The meaning of carnival's self-assertion had changed, from a protest against mob racism by conjuring joyous associations with a distant land to confrontation with the representatives of state order by claiming the right to proclaim and celebrate an alternative view of British-born identity. Radical and criminal elements which in different ways threatened the event were successfully curbed to enable the Notting Hill Carnival Trust to take over its administration, cultivating corporate sponsorship which critics thought alien to the spirit of carnival but also resisting pressures to relocate it to Hyde Park or Wormwood Scrubs.[13]

Sir Hugh Casson

Casson (1910-99) first became famous as Director of Architecture for the 1951 Festival of Britain, for which he was knighted. In 1953 he became a founder member of the Kensington Society and in that same year also became Professor of Interior Design at the Royal College of Art. He was responsible, with his architectural partner Neville Conder, for designing the adaptation of the ruins of Holland House into the King George VI Youth Hostel. His long career was marked by a versatility which ranged from designing domestic interiors for the Royal Family to designing sets for Glyndebourne. He also produced books on Oxford, Cambridge and London, illustrated with his own watercolours. After retiring

21. *Self-dramatising G K Chesterton, with toy theatre.*

from the Royal College. in 1975, Sir Hugh became President of the Royal Academy (1976-84) and moved to 60 Elgin Crescent in 1980. He continued to write, producing books on Japan and the Tower of London.[14]

Anna Maria Charretie

Thrown on her own resources by the death of her husband in 1868 Mrs Charretie (1819-75) survived by making copies of paintings in the National Gallery. She lived at Horton Cottage, 8 Hornton Street.

G K Chesterton

Chesterton (1874-1936) was born at No. 32 Sheffield Terrace. The Chestertons were old-established up-market local estate agents (still in business). The family moved on in 1877 after G K's sister Beatrice died at eight. Chesterton grew up (1877-

1901) at 11 Warwick Gardens, devouring the histories of Lord Macaulay *(qv)* and becoming "fascinated by the district of Kensington (which) was, and is, laid out like a chart to illustrate Macaulay's essays". In 1901 Chesterton married his wife Frances in St Mary Abbots *(qv)*. Chesterton claimed to have found the inspiration for his first (1904) novel while "wandering about the streets telling (himself) stories of feudal sallies and sieges". Campden Hill's lofty waterworks tower *(qv)* supplied him with the notion of a military objective and the obsolete weaponry in a local curio shop with the means to undertake it – "something irrationally arrested and pleased my eye about the look of one small block of little lighted shops and I amused myself with the suggestion that these alone were to be preserved and defended like a hamlet in a

desert and the first fantastic notion of *The Napoleon of Notting Hill* rushed over my mind." This absurdist fable, set in 1984, pictures an England governed by rulers picked at random from the civil service, regardless of suitability. Adam Wayne, Provost of Notting Hill, dares to oppose the intended assault on his cherished neighbourhood of "modern improvers with their boards and inspectors and surveyors". The novel enabled the author to develop what were to become characteristic themes in his writing – the celebration of the little man and a nostalgically conceived Merry England of beef and beer and a loathing for bureaucracy, technology and big business which prefigures the dystopia Orwell *(qv)* located in the same future year.

Chesterton also published a biography of G F Watts *(qv)* in 1904 and in 1906 an acclaimed biography of Dickens. Of Chesterton's prodigious literary output (100 volumes) the stories of the intuitive Catholic priest-detective, Father Brown, have proved most durable. Translated to the screen, the hero was skilfully personified by the suitably self-effacing Alec Guinness.

The author was himself received into the Roman church in 1922. Chesterton Road is named after him. In Martin Amis's *London Fields* (1989) Keith Talent grows up in a low-rent basement flat in Chesterton Road.[15]

22. *Rillington Place. The street was demolished when Westway was built.*

John Christie

A former choirboy, Boy Scout and Great War veteran, John Reginald Halliday Christie (1899-1953) was sacked from two jobs for dishonesty before serving time for stealing postal orders when he was a postman. Deserting his wife in his native Yorkshire in 1923, Christie came to London and went to prison twice more for theft and was convicted twice more for violence. After ten years apart Christie was rejoined by his wife in a flat at 10 Rillington Place, a short cul-de-sac. Incredibly in view of his criminal record Christie served as a reserve policeman at Harrow Road during World War Two and won two commendations. While living at Rillington Place Christie murdered at least seven women, including his wife, in order to commit acts of peri-necrophilia.

Christie was also responsible for a grotesque miscarriage of justice when in 1950 his false testimony condemned to the gallows his mentally deficient neighbour Timothy Evans, an illiterate Welshman, for the supposed murder of his wife (for whom Christie had attempted an abortion which proved fatal)

and of Evans' infant child. Christie abandoned his home and became a vagrant until his successor at Rillington Place discovered the body of one of his victims, one of three papered over in a wall recess. Christie was arrested near Putney Bridge, tried and hanged. Rillington Place was renamed Rushton Close and then demolished in the course of constructing Westway (qv). Its approximate location is now marked by Bartle Street and Rushton Mews. Evans was granted a posthumous pardon in 1966, thanks largely to the efforts of broadcaster and author Ludovic Kennedy whose book *10 Rillington Place* proved influential in changing Parliamentary opinion in favour of abolishing the death penalty. The same title was used for American director Richard Fleischer's film version of Christie's story (1971), with Sir Richard Attenborough chillingly in the name part and John Hurt as a reproachfully pathetic Evans. The film was shot in the house next door to No. 10 before demolition.[16]

The Churchill Arms

The original pub, known as the Bedford Arms, was built *c*.1824 but adopted its present name soon afterwards – i.e. well before the birth of Sir Winston – possibly as a contraction of Church Hill. Ted Bruning asserts in *London by Pub* that the pub was originally called the Marlborough after Sir Winston's famous ancestor, John Churchill, Duke of Marlborough whose greatest victory is commemorated a mile northwards in the name of Blenheim Crescent. The decor features large collections of Churchilliana, chamber pots, pot plants and butterflies. *The Evening Standard* selected it as its Pub of the Year in 1999.

23. *The Churchill Arms, photographed in November 2004.*

24. Notting Hill Gate station in 1868. The original station was opened on the Metropolitan/Circle line that year. The Central Line station was opened in 1900 and an interchange was established in 1959.

Circle Line

The Metropolitan Railway's Circle Line was extended from Westminster to Edgware Road in 1868, with a station at Nottting Hill Gate.

Clement Talbot Cars

The Clement Talbot company was founded in 1903 with the patronage and financing of the Earl of Shrewsbury and Talbot to import the French-made Clement motor car. In Barlby Road the firm developed Britain's first purpose-built car factory, constructed of reinforced concrete. The earliest models produced there were assembled from imported French parts. Production of a domestic 16 horse power model began in 1905. Record-breaking soon became a potent mode of advertising the worth of the company's output. In 1908 a 25 h.p. Talbot made the first motor crossing of Australia from Adelaide to Darwin. In 1913 Percy Lambert drove a 25 horse-power Talbot 100 miles within the hour at Brooklands. During the First World War the company switched to building ambulances and armoured cars. In 1916 the outstanding Swiss engineer Georges Roesch joined the company. Talbot was taken over by Darracq (Paris-based but British-controlled) in 1919 and in 1920 this joint company amalgamated with Sunbeam. During the 1920s Roesch originated a range of highly competitive sporting models. In 1935 the firm became part of the Rootes group and the original Talbot crest became the Sunbeam badge. All Sunbeam-Talbots were built at Barlby Road until World War Two. During that war the factory repaired Spitfire engines. The building was later used as a television studio. It was still standing in 1991 but subsequently demolished to make way for a housing estate – hence Rootes Drive. The administration building remains.[17]

Alfred Clint

Son and pupil of George Clint ARA, Alfred Clint (1807-83) was a popular marine painter and etcher. He died in his house, 54 Lancaster Road, and was buried in Kensal Green in the same grave as his father. George Clint painted a portrait of Madame Vestris *(qv)*.

Kelso Cochrane

Around 1 am on Sunday 17th May 1959 Antiguan carpenter Kelso Cochrane, walking home from St Mary's Hospital, Paddington, where his broken thumb had been plastered, was the victim of an unprovoked attack by six white teenagers which left him fatally stabbed. Despite the fact that the crime was witnessed, that names were sent to the police and that some youths were held overnight, no one was arrested or charged – despite also the fact that followers of Oswald Mosley *(qv)* openly boasted of the murder. Claudia Jones *(qv)* led a delegation to Home Secretary R A Butler, who rejected accusations of police partiality. Over 1,200 people

25. Kelso Cochrane's funeral.

of all races attended Cochrane's funeral in a gesture of anti-racist solidarity.

George Vicat Cole RA

George Vicat Cole (1833-93) lived at 8 Victoria Road, Kensington from 1868 and at Little Campden House (qv) from 1874 until his death. Taught by his artist father, he struggled initially until finding a healthy market for landscapes of the Surrey countryside and later of the Thames as a whole. His son was junior co-founder of the Byam Shaw School (qv).

Community Action

For an area which has struck many casual visitors as house-bound and inward-looking, the locality has a long, if discontinuous, history of community action, involving participants from both ends of the social spectrum. The closure of the Hippodrome racecourse (qv) might in part be attributed to the incursion of what the Sunday Times referred to disparagingly as "a more filthy or disgusting crew than ... we have seldom had the misfortune to encounter", many of them doubtless occupants of Notting Dale's Potteries (qv). The Kensington Gazette campaigned for a decade for the abolition of Notting Hill's turnpike gates, finally achieved in 1864. Squatters were a recurrent feature of Notting Hill life in the post-war period, occupying deserted or requisitioned homes in the 1940s, taking possession of Elgin Avenue properties in

the 1970s, when their numbers included Joe Strummer of The Clash, and, most imaginatively, establishing the Republic of Frestonia (qv). The Campden Hill Preservation Society was formed in 1949 in a vain attempt to save the Regency mansions of that area; campaigns to save the Water Tower and pumping station likewise failed but restrictions on the development of Holland Park School were achieved. The establishment of the Victorian Society, with its first headquarters in the former home of Linley Sambourne (qv), has proved of national, rather than merely local, significance, as has the North Kensington Law Centre opened in 1970 as Britain's first. Notting Hill's celebrated carnival (qv) can be seen as a positive community response to the racism of the 'Riots' and has been enlarged by the activities of organisations such as the Tabernacle (qv). The fracas which led to the trial of the Mangrove Nine (qv) originated in a protest against police harassment. In the 1970s the Golborne Neighbourhood Council, the first of its kind in Britain, was established to demand that redevelopment of the neighbourhood should not involve relocation of its residents elsewhere but rehousing in the locality. In 1973 the Architect's Journal praised the resulting project "for breaking new ground in techniques of public participation". Organisations to assist the welfare of specific groups can be traced back to the efforts of Mrs Bayley (qv) and the missionising of the

gypsies (qv) of Notting Dale. In more recent times they are represented by El Hogar Español, established to help refugees from the Spanish civil war, the Moroccan Women's Group and the centre for asylum-seekers from Eritrea and Ethiopia.[18]

Confined to Barracks

Litellus Burrell (1753-1827) rose from private to major-general in the service of the East India Company until, his health broken, he retired in 1821 to spend his last years at Notting Hill.

Sir John Fox Burgoyne (1782-1871) was a master of creating (and destroying) fortifications. His active career stretched from the Peninsular war to the Crimea and was rich in hon-

26. The statue of Sir John Burgoyne in Waterloo Place, sculpted by Sir Joseph Boehm.

ours – a baronetcy, the freedom of the City of London, a DCL from Oxford, the Legion d'Honneur and the rank of field-marshal. Yet all his pride was in his son, Hugh, a naval captain and one of the first men to win the VC. When Hugh was lost at sea in 1870, Burgoyne felt his purpose gone, dying a year later at 5 Pembridge Square. A statue of Burgoyne by Sir Joseph Boehm stands in Waterloo Place *(ill 26)*.

General Sir John Mark Frederick Smith FRS (1790-1874) was a distinguished sapper who became a courtier, MP and an expert on Britain's burgeoning railway system. He died at his home, 62 Pembridge Villas.

Lt-General Sir Michael White (1791-1868) fought Mahrattas, Afghans and Sikhs and had two horses shot from under him before ending his days peacefully at 15 Pembridge Crescent.

General Sir George Bell (1794-1877) fought in the Peninsular war, Burma, Canada, Gibraltar, the Caribbean and the Crimea before retiring to write his gossipy memoirs at 156 Westbourne Terrace.

Admiral Sir William Hutcheon Hall FRS (1797-1878) was an early expert on steam navigation, seeing action in China and the Crimea before retiring to 48 Phillimore Gardens.

Sir Walter Cope

A career public servant of scholarly tastes, Cope (d.1614) was an MP by 1588 and a member of the Elizabethan Society of Antiquar-

27. *The Coronet at Notting Hill Gate, c.1905.*

ies. Knighted by James VI and I on his accession, Cope as Chamberlain of the Exchequer (1609) helped to catalogue its records, then secured the offices of Keeper of Hyde Park (1610) and Master of the Wards and Liveries (1612). Meanwhile he had acquired scattered Kensington properties to consolidate them into a large estate – in 1591 West Town, in 1599 the manor of St. Mary Abbots and in 1610 Earls Court. The E-shaped house he began building around 1605 was initially known as Cope House or Cope's Castle. John Thorpe's design incorporated many up to date features, being raised above a basement, topped with an ogee turret and flanked with loggias. Cope died £27,000 in debt. The house passed to his daughter, Isobel, his sole heir, and on her marriage to Henry Rich, Earl of Holland, was renamed Holland House *(qv)*.

The Coronet

Opened in 1898 as a "theatre of which the whole County of London may be proud", the Coronet had become a cinema by 1916. As a theatre it did, however, have its days, or rather nights, of glory. Built for the impresario Edward George Saunders to the designs of WGR Sprague, it was intended to seat 1,143 and boasted six boxes and a crush bar. Stars who appeared on the stage of the Coronet included the ageing, one-legged Sarah Bernhardt, Ellen Terry, Henry Irving, Lily Langtry and Mrs. Patrick Campbell, who lived in Kensington Square and was the original Eliza Dolittle in Shaw's *Pygmalion*. In 1950 the Coronet was rebranded as a Gaumont. In the 1970s it successfully, if narrowly, resisted complete closure to figure self-referencingly in the 1991 film *Notting Hill (qv)*.

28. Walter Crane's house in Holland Street.

29. Sir William Crookes.

30. Crookes' house in Kensington Park Gardens.

Walter Crane (1845-1915)

Apprenticed as an engraver, Crane graduated to illustrating children's books and developed into a versatile designer of tiles, wallpaper, ceramics (for Wedgwood) and furniture in the manner of his mentor, William Morris. In 1881 he designed the decor and costumes for Gilbert and Sullivan's *Patience* which satirised the Aesthetic movement of which he was himself a representative type. In 1888 he was instrumental in founding the Arts and Crafts Exhibition Society, of which he was the first president. Crane served as Principal of the Royal College of Art in 1898-9 and lived at Old House, 13 Holland Street from 1892 until his death. Crane's archive was acquired by the University of Manchester.

A J Cronin (1896-1981)

After qualifying in midwifery and public health, Archibald Joseph Cronin was appointed a medical inspector of mines at 28. He produced reports on dust inhalation and first aid while in effect gathering material which he would incorporate into his highly successful novels about idealistic doctors battling against the economic and social odds. In 1926 Cronin moved to London and practised as a general practitioner at 152 Westbourne Grove. In his fifth novel, *The Citadel* (1937) he described it as "A tall leaden hued house with a surgery at the side and a brick garage behind." Cronin sold up and moved out in 1930 owing to ill health. His first novel, *Hatter's Castle* (1931) brought overnight fame, enabling him to give up medicine in favour of writing. *The Citadel* attacked the greed of the Harley Street elite and, launched with a brilliant publicity campaign by his publisher Victor Gollancz *(qv)*, created a more favourable climate of opinion for the realisation of a National Health Service.

Cronin's work is best known now through *Dr. Finlay's Casebook* which became a popular television series. Cronin's practice survives as the Garway Road Medical Centre.[19]

Sir William Crookes

A gentleman scientist who financed his own experiments, Crookes (1832-1919) discovered the element thallium in 1861 and was consequently elected FRS when only 31. In 1880 Crookes moved into 7 Kensington Park Gardens, setting up a laboratory for himself in the basement, where he discovered what are now known as cathode rays. Crookes' house is claimed to be the first in London to have electricity. He certainly made his own tungsten filament lamps and by 1891 was a director of the Notting Hill Electric Light Company. Crookes also conducted a five year investigation of spiritualists and mediums, organising seances which attracted other interested personalities including Darwin (*qv*), Madame Blavatsky, Conan Doyle and Houdini. Knighted in 1897, he became President of the Royal Society in 1913. He also invented the spectroscope and the radiometer, founded *Chemical News* (1859) and edited the *Quarterly Journal of Science*.

William Crotch

A self-taught musical prodigy, Crotch (1775-1847) could play the piano, organ and violin by the age of seven and was appointed organist of Christ Church, Oxford at fifteen. Resigning the professorship of music which he had held since 1797, Crotch came to London *c*.1810, being in great demand as a teacher. In 1822 he was appointed first principal of the Royal Academy of Music. Apart from a set of ten anthems, Crotch also published his Oxford lectures on music. A keen artist and friend of Constable, Crotch made many pictures of the area around his home (1821-31) at "No. 1 High Street, Notting Hill, Kensington Gravel Pits", which stood opposite the entrance to Kensington Church Street (then Silver Street). These include views of *Norland House, Sunset on Cambden (sic) Hill,* his own house, the view from his bedroom window and a terrace near Addison Road. In 1831 Crotch moved to 10 Holland Street.

Robert Needham Cust

After losing two wives while working as an imperial ad-

31. *Charles Darwin.*

ministrator in India, Cust (1821-1909) retired to Campden Hill Road to produce some sixty volumes on Asian and African languages and comparative religion.

Darwin's Dealings

Charles Darwin never lived in North Kensington but he had several friends who did. Between 1862 and 1865 Alfred Russell Wallace (1823-1913) wrote Darwin at least a dozen letters from 5 Westbourne Grove Terrace, sending him papers on Malaysian parrots, wild honeycomb from Timor and flowers from Singapore and setting forth his own views on such topics as the abortive wings of the ostrich and the muscular fibres of bees. In 1867 Wallace wrote from 76 Westbourne Grove about his dispute with the dotty Duke of Argyll (*qv*). In the same year the Scottish entomologist Andrew Murray (1812-78) wrote to Darwin from 67 Bedford Gardens to inform him of a new natural history publication he was planning. In 1869 M L Ruck

of 13 Kensington Park Road corresponded with Darwin on the development of horns in sheep. Between 1870 and 1872 Darwin received at least five letters from W W Reade (*qv*) of 11 St Mary Abbot's Terrace on topics ranging from ideas of female beauty to the Spartans. In 1871 G J Allman (*qv*) of 15 Campden Hill Road sent Darwin proof sheets of his monograph on the descent of tubularian hydroids from graptolites. In 1872 neurologist Armand de Watteville (1846-1925) wrote from Grove House, Pembridge Square to advise Darwin of the publication date of an early French anthropological treatise which he was trying to trace. In 1874 the Scottish anthropologist John Ferguson McLennan (1827-81) then living on Campden Hill, wrote to ask Darwin for a paper on marriage in primitive societies. In 1877 P Hodgskin of 20 Linden Gardens sent Darwin the nest of a Uruguayan bird. In the same year Darwin sent a congratulatory letter to Sara Sedgwick of 23 Elgin Crescent on the occasion of her engagement to his son William.

Sir Edmund Davis (1862-1939)

Australian-born mining millionaire Davis, having made a fortune in South Africa, moved into 11 Lansdowne Road when he was just twenty-seven, hiring Charles Conder (1868-1909) and Frank Brangwyn (1867-1956), both in their early twenties, to give the house an aesthetic make-over. Early aficionados of the work of Rodin, Davis

32. A scene from The Lighthouse, performed at Campden House, in which Charles Dickens and Wilkie Collins participated.

33. Charles Dickens

and his wife had Lansdowne House *(qv)* built in 1900 as an artists' colony. Their art collection was bequeathed to museums in Paris and South Africa. The house was from 1947 to 1983 a residential club for the Catholic Knights of St Columba.

Denbigh Close

Poet Christopher Logue lived here in the 1960s and described it in his memoir *Prince Charming*. No. 18 was the bachelor pad occupied by Charlie Croker (Michael Caine) in the original version of *The Italian Job*.

Dickens Family

Charles Dickens (1812-70) was so horrified by the condition of Notting Dale during the cholera epidemic of 1849 that he published an account of it (by W H Wills) in the very first edition of his magazine *Household Words*. Dickens was a regular member of the literary coterie which foregathered regularly

at Holland House *(qv)* and was often a guest at Moray Lodge *(qv)*. An accomplished amateur actor, in July 1855 Dickens took part in a charity performance of his friend Wilkie Collins' *The Lighthouse* staged at Campden House *(qv)*. In 1865 he read from his work at Aubrey House *(qv)* to entertain the visiting American writer Louisa May Alcott. Dickens was also an early patron of Marcus Stone *(qv)*. Dickens' great-granddaughter, the novelist Monica Dickens (1915-93), grew up at 52 Chepstow Villas. Her memoir *An Open Book* contains a description of Portobello Road *(qv)* market as seen through the eyes of a child in the 1920s.

As a Kensington councillor in the 1950s Monica's father, Henry Dickens, was responsible for the building of the blocks of council flats collectively named Henry Dickens Court in his honour and individually named after characters in his grandfather's novels.

Sir Frank Dicksee

Francis Bernard Dicksee (1853-1928), son of the painter and etcher Thomas Francis Dicksee, is remembered for literary and historical subjects like *Romeo and Juliet* or *The Passing of Arthur*. Painted in a Pre-Raphaelite mode, many became well known as book illustrations. Dicksee's

34. 80 Peel Street, studio of Sir Frank Dicksee, and later of William Russell Flint.

studio at 80 Peel Street had been built in 1876 for the landscape painter Matthew Ridley Corbett (1850-1902). It was taken over by Sir William Russell Flint *(qv)*. Dicksee's uncle, John Robert Dicksee (1817-1905) taught Linley Sambourne *(qv)*.

Frank Dillon (1823-1909)
A landscape artist, Dillon (1823-1909) travelled in Egypt several times, lived in Japan in 1876-7, and campaigned for conservation in Cairo and Venice. He was also a close friend of Mazzini and helped Kossuth *(qv)* in his exile. Dillon was living at 13 Upper Phillimore Gardens by 1861 and died there.

Ashley Dukes
Trained as a scientist, Dukes (1885-1959) became a drama critic then a dramatist, drawing on his extensive knowledge of German and French theatre. During the Great War he rose from private to major in the Machine Gun Corps. Dukes married Marie Rambert *(qv)* in 1918 and returned to drama criticism and adapting German plays. He opened the Mercury Theatre *(qv)* in 1933, brought Vivien Leigh to the West End stage and in his 1942 work *The Scene is Changed* produced what has been called "his one not very factual venture into autobiography". Between 1945 and 1949 Dukes headed Britain's efforts to re-establish the drama, music and cultural activities in its zone of occupied Germany.

Edmund Dulac
Educated as a scientist and trained as an artist in his native Toulouse, Dulac (1882-1953) settled in London at 23. Initially specialising as an illustrator of fairy tales, he subsequently branched out into cartoons, costume design, magazine covers and portraiture, including witty caricatures of Kitchener, Churchill, Sir Thomas Beecham and Lawrence Binyon. Dulac also designed stage scenery, the King's poetry prize medal and celebratory stamps for the coronations of 1937 and 1953. Despite being naturalised as British he used his art to raise money for the French Red Cross in World War One and during World War Two devised currency and stamps for the Free French cause. It was thanks to an introduction by Dulac that the very youthful Constant Lambert became the first English composer to be commissioned by Diaghilev. A perfectionist craftsman, he was also an expert cook and marksman and connoisseur of Oriental art. Dulac lived at Studio House, Ladbroke Grove and 72 Ladbroke Road.

Electric Cinema
Designed by Gerald Seymour Valentin (missing, presumed dead, at the Battle of Loos in 1915), the Electric Cinema on Portobello Road was one of the earliest (1910-11) purpose-built cinemas in Britain, certainly London's oldest and the earliest still operating, incorporating the stringent new safety standards re-

35. *The Electric Cinema.*

quired by the 1909 Cinematograph Act. Despite a spell as a musical hall, known from 1919 as the Imperial Playhouse, and despite long periods of disuse and neglect, it has remained virtually unaltered. The building was made the subject of a preservation order in 1972 and is a Grade II* listed structure, characterised by English Heritage as "the quintessential and most ravishingly pretty cinema of its period". After a £5,000,000+ refit it reopened in 2001. Saviour Peter Simon once ran a market stall opposite – until he became head of the Monsoon and Acessorize retail chains. The cinema changed hands again a year later and gained a brasserie and private members' club. Capacity has been cut from 600 to 240 to accommodate luxury armchairs.

Elgin Crescent
Built up in the 1850s the imposing mansions of Elgin Crescent were promoted as 'Handsomely Finished' nine-

36. Katherine Mansfield, who lived in Elgin Crescent. From a painting by Anne Estelle Rice.

37. 31 Melbury Road, home of Luke Fildes.

bedroomed 'Family Residences' with rear access to "ornamental pleasure grounds" and with "omnibuses within a few minutes walk" – all for an annual rent ranging from £60 to £80. Part of the gardens was given over to a tennis club where Wimbledon champion Fred Perry played.

No. 95 was briefly the home of New Zealand short story writer Katherine Mansfield (1888-1923). Laurence Olivier (1907-89) lived at No. 86 in the 1920s. Osbert Lancaster *(qv)* was born and grew up at No. 79.

In July and August 1884 Madame Blavatsky, founder of the Theosophical Society, was the house-guest at No. 77; half a century later her hostess Francesca Arundale published an account of this interlude, recording examples of Blavatsky's supposed supernatural powers. Nehru *(qv)* lodged at No. 60. Novelist Emma Tennant (1938-) was a long-term resident. Elgin Books, opened in 1980, although much favoured by local literati, closed in 2000.

Elm Lodge

Built *c.* 1810 and demolished in 1878 to make way for the construction of Airlie Gardens, Elm Lodge stood adjacent to Thorpe Lodge on Campden Hill. Its most illustrious inhabitant was Sir James McGrigor FRS (1771-1858), head of Wellington's medical services during the Peninsular War and founder of the Royal Army Medical Corps.

Thomas Faed

A fellow pupil of Erskine Nicol *(qv)*, Faed (1826-1900) specialised in sentimental Scottish genre subjects (eg *A Mitherless Bairn*, *The Last of the Clans*), popular with a public which shared their monarch's rapture for the Highlands. In 1870 Faed was living at Sussex Villa, Campden Hill.

Sir William Fairbairn

Fairbairn (1789-1874) became one of the earliest residents of Holland Park, shortly after he had been created a baronet. A Scot who had invented a steam excavator and a sausage-making machine, neither to much purpose, he prospered with a locomotive and textile machinery works in Manchester and a shipyard at Millwall and by making the tubular iron components for Robert Stephenson's great bridges at Conway and over the Menai Straits.

Sir (Samuel) Luke Fildes

A product of the South Kensington and Royal Academy Art Schools, Fildes (1844-1927) progressed from magazines to illustrations for Dickens' unfinished novel *The Mystery of Edwin Drood* and on to large-scale canvases with a social agenda, enjoying his first great success with

Applicants for admission to a Casual Ward (1874). Fildes' marriage to the sister of artist Henry Woods, based in Venice, turned him to Italian subjects. Royal Academician from 1887 and for many years chairman of the Arts Club, Fildes attained his greatest popularity with *The Doctor* (1891), now in the Tate Gallery. Reconstructing a dingy fisherman's cottage in his studio, Fildes depicted a devoted physician's vigil at the bedside of a child. For decades afterwards engravings of this tribute to the medical profession hung in the waiting-rooms of countless doctors. (Fildes had been bombarded with offers from practitioners seeking to pose in the part but preferred to use a professional model.) Turning to portraiture Fildes was commissioned to produce the official coronation portrait of Edward VII, followed by official portraits of Queen Alexandra and George V, for which undertakings he was knighted and created GCVO (Fildes' own portrait was painted by Philip de Laszlo (*qv*)).

Fildes' imposing house at No. 31 (until 1967 No. 11) Melbury Road was designed for him in 1876 by R Norman Shaw (*qv*) (who deemed the site 'delicious') in a style described by Pevsner as "Queen Anne of the utmost precision". It cost £4,500. Fildes, who had shared a Paris studio with Marcus Stone (*qv*) in 1874, thought his residence "a long way the most superior house of the whole lot; I consider it knocks Stone's to fits ...". (Even Edward VII was impressed

when he came as a sitter to the centrally-heated studio). Fildes lived there until his death. The house was for a while converted into flats. At the time of writing it is the home of the film-maker Michael Winner.

Sir William Russell Flint
The son, brother and father of artists, Flint (1880-1969) was trained for the printing trade and first worked as a medical illustrator before being taken on by the *Illustrated London News* and the Medici Society. Versatile in subject-matter, from muscular nudes to landscapes, adept in oils or water-colour, he was neither controversial nor experimental but did have a penchant for painting gypsies – the Spanish kind rather than the Notting Dale variety. Flint lived at 80 Peel Street from 1924 until his death.[20]

Ford Madox Ford
"I learned all I know of Literature from Conrad – and England has learned all it knows of Literature from me." On himself.

The grandson of the Pre-Raphaelite artist Ford Madox Brown and son of music critic Francis Hueffer, Ford (1873-1939) was registered at birth as Ford Hermann Hueffer, adopted the additional names Joseph Leopold Madox and in 1919 changed his surname by deed poll to Ford. His love life was no less complicated. In 1894 Ford eloped with and married Elsie Martindale, by whom he had two daughters and with whom he lived at 10 Airlie Gardens. In 1910 an order was made against him

38. *Ford Madox Ford.*

for restitution of conjugal rights. By then the novelist Violet Hunt, wayward daughter of the painter, W T Hunt (*qv*), had become Ford's mistress. In 1931 Elsie successfully sued the *Throne* newspaper for describing Violet as Mrs Ford Madox Hueffer. In the same year James Joyce (*qv*) wrote:

> *"O Father O'Ford, you've a masterful way with you, Maid, wife and widow are wild to make hay with you ..."*

Ford's first major publications were biographies of Ford Madox Brown and Rossetti. He then collaborated with Joseph Conrad in the writing of three novels. Ford considered the best of his eighty books to be his novel *The Good Soldier: A Tale of Passion* (1915), which is about passion, not soldiering and was described as "the finest French novel in the English language". Ford's greater literary contribution was through his essays and criticism and in particular through the *English Review* which he founded in 1908. The first issue featured H G Wells' *Tono Bungay* and included contributions from Henry James and Tolstoy. Hardy, Conrad and Galsworthy *(qv)* were among later contributors and Ezra Pound *(qv)*, Wyndham Lewis *(qv)* and D H Lawrence were among Ford's 'discoveries' but the magazine's cultural impact was not matched by commercial success. Within a year Ford was forced to sell his collection of his grandfather's paintings. During this period (from 1907 to 1910) he lived in a maisonette above a poultry and fishmonger's shop at 84 Holland Park Avenue. South Lodge, No. 80 Campden Hill Road, was Violet Hunt's address from *c*.1908 until 1942; Ford stayed there as her 'paying guest' between 1913 and 1919. (Wyndham Lewis added some avant-garde touches to the decor, such as decorating Ford's writing room a violent red. He also described Ford with characteristic spite as "a flabby lemon and pink giant" in his appropriately titled *Rude Assignment*. From 1915 to 1917 Ford (then still Hueffer) served as an officer with the Welch Regiment and was invalided home after being severely gassed. Returning to London he lived at 20A Campden Hill Gardens, a single-room studio flat, in 1919, the year in which he changed his name (to the mockery of Pound who called him 'Forty Mad-dogs Whoofer', which was kinder than Osbert Sitwell's 'Freud

Madox Fraud'). In 1922 Ford moved to Paris, founded the *Transatlantic Review* and divided the rest of his life between France and the USA.[21]

Charles Richard Fox

The illegitimate son of the third Lord Holland, Fox (1796-1873) served in the navy and then the Grenadiers, eventually becoming a general. Variously also a Member of Parliament and a courtier, he was most distinguished as a numismatist, amassing a collection of 11,500 Greek coins (now in Berlin). His house at Addison Road *(qv)* was a meeting-place for archaeologists.

Frestonia

Surrounded by dereliction and faced with the threat of displacement to make way for the comprehensive 'redevelopment' of their street in 1977 the squatters of Freston Road seceded from the UK and appealed to the UN to send peacekeepers to forestall their eviction by the GLC. Inspired by the 1948 Ealing Studios comedy *Passport to Pimlico*, the street's 120 residents eschewed the office of prime minister but granted a ministerial portfolio to any willing office-holder – the Minister of State for Education was a two-year-old. They also issued postage stamps and visas, adopted a national anthem and established a National Theatre and National Film Institute. As an affirmation of solidarity Frestonians (motto *Nos sumus una familia* – We are one family) unanimously adopted the

cognomen Bramley, trusting that this would oblige the GLC to rehouse them all together. TV crews and tourists were attracted from Japan, New Zealand and Denmark. The GLC prudently accepted the verdict of a public enquiry and "Frestonia was eventually rebuilt ... with several millions of pounds of foreign aid from Great Britain, channelled via the Notting Hill Housing Trust." The 21st anniversary of 'independence' was marked by a party in the communal garden. In 1984 Nicholas Albery (1949-2001), one of Frestonia's moving spirits, enlisted the support of Edward de Bono, Anita Roddick and Fay Weldon to establish The Institute for Social Inventions which developed such practices as child-to-child counselling in primary schools. Albery was also a promoter of the Neal's Yard wholefood complex and of DIY burials and compiler of the bestselling *Poem For the Day* anthology. Ironically Albery, an inveterate hiker and the author of the *Time Out Book of Country Walks*, who never himself owned a car, was killed in a car crash.[22]

William Powell Frith

Frith (1819-1909) moved into 7 (then 10) Pembridge Villas in 1852. Despite a humble background and poor education, he had attained admission to the Royal Academy Schools and by 21 was painting subjects drawn from English literature, especially Shakespeare and Dickens. Genre work followed and in 1853 he was created RA,

39. William Powell Frith, a painter of busy canvasses.

had another seven by his mistress, Mary Alford, who lived only a mile away and whom he married after Isabelle's death in 1880. Frith's highly entertaining memoirs (1887) were frank about his commercial opportunism but his confession that it had been a toss-up whether he would become a painter or an auctioneer provoked Whistler to remark "he must have tossed up." Frith also wrote a biography of John Leech. His pupils included the prolific *Vanity Fair* portraitist Leslie Ward ('Spy'); his work inspired East Ender Mark Gertler to persevere in his ambition to become a painter. Frith's friends included the novelist Wilkie Collins; in his youth he had been a member of 'The Clique', which included Augustus Egg and Richard Dadd. The site of Frith's magnificent mansion was redeveloped as a garage in the 1930s.

(Edwin) Maxwell Fry

Described as "one of the few active Modernist architects in pre-war Britain who was actually British", Fry (1899-1987) is now remembered for his post-war work in Nigeria and India but his outstanding domestic achievement was Kensal House, built for the Gas, Light and Coke Company at Kensal Green in 1936-7. Characterised by Pevsner as a "progressive-minded" housing development, its twin linked slabs of reinforced concrete were sited so that sleepers in the bedrooms on their eastern aspect would awaken to the

enjoying huge success the following year with his meticulously observed view of the Victorian seaside *Ramsgate Sands.* Queen Victoria bought it for 1,000 guineas. This triumph was eclipsed with similar incident-packed large-scale compositions depicting *Derby Day* (1858) ("fifteen months incessant labour") and *The Railway Station* (1862), a panorama of Paddington in which he included himself and his family. Even Ruskin commended *Derby Day* as "a kind of cross between John Leech *(qv)* and Wilkie and a dash of daguerrotype here and there and some pretty seasoning with Dickens's

sentiment." Frith consequently received a royal invitation to paint the wedding of the Prince of Wales. The commission commanded a fee of £3,000 and took an entire year. In 1875 Frith's *The Dinner in Boswell's Rooms at Bond Street* was sold for £4567, the highest sum at that date ever paid for the work of a living painter. Nevertheless snooty art critics continued to accuse Frith of painting "for those who like pictures without liking art."

Frith's financial success enabled him to maintain a bourgeois lifestyle with a well-kept secret. While his wife Isabelle presented him with twelve children, Frith

40. Maxwell Fry, architect of Kensal House.

rising sun and in the evening could view its setting from their living-rooms on the western side. "Intended as a practical experiment in mass automatic fuel service to low-rental flats", the project was to epitomise the virtues of gas for heating and cooking but still featured the miniscule balconies deemed essential for air-drying the weekly wash. Much of the credit for the design and planning of the interiors of the sixty-eight flats should be given to housing reformer Elizabeth Denby (1894-1965). There were also club rooms, a laundry and a canteen for the tenants and a nursery school for their children. To promote public awareness of the project a film was made showing families first of all in their original sordid homes then in their state-of-the-art new accommodation. Fry's other local construction is the block of flats at 65 Ladbroke Gardens, built in 1938, the only listed modern building on the Ladbroke estate.[23]

41. John Galsworthy. Photo by Riess.

John Galsworthy

Galsworthy (1867-1933), the future Nobel Laureate, lived successively at South House, 82 Campden Hill Road (1897-1903), 16a Aubrey Walk (1903-5) and 14 Addison Road (1905-13). The first volume of the Forsyte Saga, *The Man of Property* appeared in the same year (1906) as his first stage success *The Silver Box*. *Justice* (1910), Galsworthy's crusading attack on the blind cruelties of prison life, moved Home Secretary Winston Churchill to initiate significant reforms. Orwell *(qv)*, however, condemned Galsworthy as "utterly unable to move his mind outside the wealthy bourgeois society he is attacking". Galsworthy served as the first president of PEN, the international writers' organisation.

The Gate Theatre

Located above the Prince Albert pub in Pembridge Road, The Gate was founded by Lou Stein in 1979 and has specialised in an international repertoire.

David Lloyd George

The former Prime Minister, David Lloyd George (1863-1945) used No. 2 Addison Road as his London base for a decade after 1928. Having renounced the leadership of the Liberal Party, during these years he concentrated on composing his self-justifying *War Memoirs* (1933-6), assisted by the *Daily Telegraph's* military expert, Captain (Sir) Basil Liddell Hart, who concurred with the ex-Premier's view that the blame for huge British losses in the Great War should be laid at the door of the generals.

Gilbert and Sullivan

W S Gilbert's boyhood home was at 14 Pembridge Gardens. Sullivan's first private rooms after leaving home

42. Caricature of Gilbert and Sullivan in 1878.

43. In memoir mode – David Lloyd George. From an oil painting by Sir William Orpen.

were at 139 Westbourne Terrace. In 1868 Gilbert moved to 8 Essex Villas, off Argyll Road. Here he lived for eight years, wrote 33 plays (including *Trial by Jury*) and pursued a vendetta (mutual) with his next door neighbour over noise.[24]

John Hall Gladstone FRS

Like Crookes *(qv)* Gladstone's private means enabled him to become a prolific research chemist, producing 140 papers, plus 78 more in collaboration with others. He also pioneered science education in schools, wrote on the compatibility of science and Christianity and was a founder of the YMCA. Gladstone (1827-1902) wrote an early and popular biography of his friend Michael Faraday. Ramsay MacDonald, Britain's first Labour premier, was Gladstone's son-in-law. Gladstone died at 17 Pembridge Square.

Gloucester Walk

J M Barrie lived at No. 14 in 1892, his recently published novel *The Little Minister* having brought him his first whiff of fame. The dope-smoking Estonian Count Eric Stenbock (1860-95), a friend of More Adey *(qv)*, lived at No. 21 from 1890 until shortly before he died from a fall while trying in a drunken rage to attack someone with a poker.

Victor Gollancz

St Paul's School, New College, Oxford, the Northumberland Fusiliers, teaching at Repton School and an abortive posting to Singapore constituted Gollancz's eclectic qualifications for entering the world of publishing. Founding his own imprint in 1928 he moved into 42 Ladbroke Grove the following year. He enjoyed instant success with R C Sheriff's *Journey's End*, pioneered revolutionary typographical jackets and bargain omnibus editions, created the postal subscription Left Book Club and signed up A J Cronin *(qv)*, Ford Madox Ford *(qv)*, Daphne du Maurier, Dorothy L Sayers and George Orwell *(qv)*. A spellbinding speaker and a connoisseur collector of English pottery, in 1953, the year he left Ladbroke Grove, he was awarded the German Order of Merit for his efforts to relieve starvation in that defeated country after 1945 – which was entirely consistent with his refusal to publish the highly profitable war memoirs of Nazi generals. Gollancz (1893-1967) was also a founder member of the Campaign for Nuclear Disarmament and a campaigner against capital punishment.[25]

Kenneth Grahame

A reluctant success at the Bank of England, Grahame (1859-1932), who lived at 16 Phillimore Place, Campden Hill from 1901 to 1908, found consolation in his writing and in his adored only son, Alistair. The bedtime stories and letters composed for 'Master Mouse' became *Wind in the Willows* (1908), although never originally been intended for publication and rejected by the American

44. Victor Gollancz.

publisher who had importuned the author for a MS. The English edition received only a muted reaction but has never been out of print. In 1929 A A Milne adapted the book for the stage as *Toad of Toad Hall*. Alistair achieved his father's thwarted ambition of studying at Oxford but was killed by a train before he was twenty, almost certainly a suicide. Father and son are buried in the same grave.

Grand Junction Canal

Plans to cut a link from the Grand Junction Canal to Paddington were approved by Parliament in 1793. It was to become London's main link with the rest of the national canal system. Half a mile of the route selected cut through the farmland of Notting Barns (then known as Smith's Farm).

Opened in 1801 a first section of the canal, known as

45. *The opening of the Grand Junction Canal to Paddington in July 1801.*

46. The canal in 1804.

48. The Canal in November 2004.

the Paddington Canal, served to carry building supplies and offered leisure excursions to Greenford and Uxbridge, excursionists often being accompanied by a band.

The entire through route, leading up to the Midlands, opened in 1805. The opening of the Regent's Canal in 1820, providing a more direct link with London's docks, was a blow to the Grand Junction's commercial traffic but it retained its appeal as a summer diversion. In 1929 it became part of the Grand Union Canal system.

The canal was memorably described in 1959 by novelist and local resident Colin MacInnes *(qv)* as one "that nothing floats on except cats and contraceptives".

Margaret Drabble's novel *The Radiant Way* (1987) features a psychopath who cuts the heads off people walking beside the canal. In Michael Moorcock's *Mother London* (1988) the Scaramanga sisters live in 'Bank Cottage' (fictitious) on the south side of the canal opposite the cemetery.

The London terminus of the 'Paddington Arm' was 'dewatered' in 1999 in anticipation of major building redevelopment. In July 2003 a major boost to the canal's commercial traffic was announced with the prospect of a long-term contract to bring 450,000 tons of building materials into the capital, thereby relieving the roads of heavy lorry traffic.[26]

Gravel Pits

'Gravilpits' are recorded at Kensington in 1654 and Notting Hill is marked as Kensington Gravel Pits on the Ordnance Survey Map of 1822. Some of the pits still survived then as large ponds. An ink sketch of 1845 depicts the Swan public house as located there.

The almshouses of 1711 which stood next door to it were taken down in 1821 and Greyhound Row built on

47. The Queen's Lying-in Hospital at Kensington Gravel Pits, c1820. Watercolour, artist unknown.

49. *The almshouses at the Gravel Pits, 1821. Drawn by Robert Banks.*

their site. In 1791 farmer Henry Hayman nabbed twenty-year-old Thomas Bradley as he tried to run off with his washing; Bradley was found guilty of larceny at the Old Bailey but permitted to enlist in the army of the East India Company in lieu of punishment. Artist Sir Augustus Wall Callcott *(qv)* was born and died at Kensington Gravel Pits. Artists William Crotch, William Mulready and John Linnell *(qqv)* also lived there.

Gypsies

By the mid-nineteenth century many gypsy clans had established a pattern of travelling the countryside from spring to autumn to follow their traditional trades of dealing, mending pans and chairs or working as harvest gangs. In the winter they

50. *The Three Horseshoes near the Gravel Pits. After R H Laurie, 1795.*

settled on open ground on the fringes of London, in areas such as Wanstead or Wandsworth. By the 1860s they were regularly wintering at Kensal Green, along Latimer Road, on 'Black Hill', now part of Avondale Park and on the former brickfield where St Clement's church was to be

Latimer Road. Gypsies in caravans are enumerated in the census of 1881. Charles Booth's poverty survey of the 1890s made it clear that the winter soup kitchens organised by local churches and charities, like the one at St Agnes at the end of Bangor Street, were a major attraction for the large gypsy families. An investigator recorded of Sirdar Road, "As we passed the children were coming out of the Board School ... Many children of dark, gypsy type."

51 and 52. Gypsy encampments near Latimer Road in 1879 and 1880. From the Illustrated London News.

Hammersmith and City Line
Opened in 1864 as a feeder to the Metropolitan Line from Paddington to Farringdon, the line had a station at Notting Dale (now Ladbroke Grove) and joined the Great Western Railway at Westbourne Park. Services ran every half hour.

Hanover Lodge
Originally 8 Queen's Villas and from 1863 14 Lansdowne Road, this house was occupied by members of the Petrie family from 1855 until at least the 1970s when Professor E M Carus-Wilson (1897-1977), historian of English medieval trade, was living there.

Thomas Hardy
Having initially trained under Dorchester architect John Hicks, Hardy (1840-1928) came to London in 1862 to join Arthur Blomfield's flourishing practice. Hardy's first lodging was at 3 Clarence Place but in 1863 he moved to 16 Westbourne Park Villas. Although he was for a while

built. In 1869 a mission was established to bring Christianity to a semi-permanent gypsy community by then established at Notting Dale. Under the leadership of an ancient patriarch, Old Hearn, who claimed to be a veteran of the Napoleonic wars, many gypsies were said to have signed the pledge, given up fortune-telling and the Romany tongue, sold off their horses and accepted a settled life even to the extent of taking out hawkers' licences and becoming formally married. An outbreak of scarlet fever gave the authorities a pretext to insist that the encampment break up and move on but the pattern of over-wintering in the area persisted. In November 1879 *The Illustrated London News* published views of an encampment near

53. *Thomas Hardy, from an oil painting by Augustus John.*

cameras, concerts, cruises, pantomimes and sheep dip. Hassall's rotund, prancing fisherman proclaiming that 'Skegness is so bracing' (1908) was still in use after his death. Hassall only ever visited Skegness once, in 1936, when he was honoured for putting the town on the map. Hassall also helped Baden-Powell design the Boy Scout uniform. During the Great War he designed recruiting posters, posters for Belgian civilian relief, for YMCA huts in France and another, aimed at the Dog-Owners of Kensington, appealing to them to comb out their coats and deliver the surplus 'wool' to 30 Holland Park Road where Miss Du Cros would collect it to be made into "comforts for the sick and wounded". Ultimately rewarded with a Civil List pension, Hassall nevertheless died in poverty. His daughter Joan became a painter and his son Christopher Vernon Hassall (1912-63) became a poet and librettist. The Hassall home was in Kensington Park Road.

Sir Edward Henry

The father of finger-printing in Britain, Henry (1850-1931), Commissioner of the Metropolitan Police, lived in Sheffield Terrace (1903-20). Of Irish Catholic descent, he had served with distinction in the police service in India and South Africa, pioneering the use of finger-printing in criminal detection by devising a system for classifying fingerprints. In 1912 Alfred Bowes tried to murder Henry on the steps of his home after

a member of the congregation of St Mary Abbot's, Hardy's continuing self-education through extensive reading led him to abandon his faith and to begin writing poetry. *The Ruined Maid*, an accomplished ironic ballad about a prostitute's finery and affected manner, was composed at Westbourne Park Villas in 1866 but was not published until 1901. In 1867, low in health and spirits, Hardy returned to Dorchester and began working on his first novel. Returning to London in 1872, Hardy found

literary success with *Far From the Madding Crowd* (1874), abandoned his architectural career and married. After a short spell in Surbiton, Hardy and his bride moved to 18 Newton Road, Westbourne Grove.[27]

John Hassall

Trained in Paris and Antwerp, Hassall (1868-1948) found work as a children's book illustrator before prospering as a poster artist designing advertisements for whisky, vacuum cleaners, he had been refused a cab licence. Henry was seriously injured by one of the three shots fired by Bowes but pleaded for leniency in his sentence (life was reduced to fifteen years) and even funded his subsequent emigration to Canada. Elevated to a baronetcy, Henry modestly styled himself "of Campden House Court".

Sir George Henschel

Ultimately more celebrated as a conductor than as a composer, Henschel (1850-1934) left his native Prussia in 1877 and made his first public apppearance in Britain as a baritone, inaugurating the idea of the song recital. As Professor of Singing at the Royal College of Music he founded the London Symphony Concerts, which he conducted. Henschel lived on Campden Hill and numbered Whistler, Brahms and Burne-Jones among his friends. Henschel's portrait was painted by John Singer Sargent, Sir Lawrence Alma-Tadema and Philip de Laszlo (*qv*) a near neighbour. Henschel was unique in being the only living musician to have an entry in the first three editions of Grove's *Dictionary of Music and Musicians.* A keen amateur painter, he also wrote an autobiography *Musings and Memories* (1918).

Thomas Henshaw

Henshaw (1618-1700) spent five years at Oxford without taking a degree and studied at Middle Temple but practised little law. After serving with royalist forces, he became a major in the French army and travelled widely in Italy and Spain. By the standards of the day this amounted to a well-rounded education. After the Restoration Henshaw served as French secretary to Charles II, retaining his position under James II and William III successively. In 1663 he was chosen as one of the twenty founder Fellows of the Royal Society and later published treatises on saltpetre and gunpowder. Henshaw was regarded by some as a master of the occult and collaborated with Sir Robert Paston in the search for a mysterious 'red elixir'. A friend of the diarist John Evelyn and royal physician, Sir Hans Sloane, Henshaw shared their passion for gardening and plants and exchanged seeds with them. Henshaw also served as ambassador in Denmark for over two years and translated an Italian history of China. He lived for half a century, and died, at a house on the Holland House estate, near a group of ponds known as the Moats. Kensington antiquary Thomas Faulkner believed the house (largely demolished in 1801 and the remainder used as a gardener's cottage) had been the manor house of West Town.

Baptist Hicks, 1st Viscount Campden

Third son of a rich Cheapside mercer of Gloucestershire descent, Hicks (1551-1629) supplied the royal court and, to general amazement, unashamedly continued to keep shop even after being knighted by King James. Contemporaries attributed fabulous wealth to him, hailing him as one "who knew how to amass money as a merchant and spend it as a prince". Stow alleged that Hicks married off both his daughters, one to a baronet, the other to a lord, with a fortune of £100,000 each. He was also one of the sponsors of the settlement of Jamestown, Virginia. In 1608 Hicks bought the manor of Campden, Gloucs. where he built a house, the façade of which was said to have cost £29,000. (It was burned to ruins by royalists in 1645.) In 1609 he bought "a capital messuage and two closes known as the Racks and King's Mead" from the Crown. In 1616 he added another seventy acres adjacent and on this site began to build what became Campden House (*qv*), in rivalry to the recently deceased Sir Walter Cope (*qv*). As he was generous in his loans to the Stuart monarchy he was created baronet in 1620 and elevated to the peerage in 1628 as Baron Hicks of Ilmington, Warwickshire and Viscount Campden. He left £200 for the poor of Kensington. Augmented by a further £200 from his widow and £150 from Oliver Cromwell, this rather modest bequest from "a very harsh man" became the multi-million pound Campden Charities (*qv*).

Highway Robbery

In 1734 highwayman James MacDowald held up a stagecoach at Kensington Gravel Pits, was apprehended, found guilty and hanged. In 1736

54 and 55. Scenes at the Hippodrome c.1838.

Charles Serjeant was stripped of everything except his wig and tied to a tree in a field by "the first bridge, a little below Notting Hill". One assailant, William Rine, was caught, confessed and was hanged. In 1772 Lady Mary Coke of Aubrey Lodge recorded hearing a highwayman being shot outside her grounds. In 1774 Francis Bowkett was robbed at pistol point by two men "about the middle of Notting Hill"; one subsequently denounced the other, who was hanged.

The Hippodrome

Notting Hill would have been a good place to have a race course – if there hadn't been a public footpath over it. As the nearest alternative course was at Epsom, it might reasonably expect to draw large crowds from fashionable Marylebone and rapidly growing Bayswater. The hill itself, now surmounted by the church of St John the Evangelist (qv), offered a splendid vantage point from which spectators could view an entire race as competitors followed the course laid out below them. In 1836 John Whyte was granted a twenty-one-year lease, laid out courses for both flat racing and steeplechasing and erected a formal entrance at what is now the junction of Pembridge Road and Kensington Park Road. He also enlisted representatives of the beau monde as stewards – the Earl of Chesterfield and the foppish Count D'Orsay. The first races were run on 3rd June 1837 but by then Whyte was already facing legal action and an unruly mob successfully demanded free entrance. Undaunted, Whyte eventually altered the course to avoid the footpath, re-sited the entrance, fenced it in and promised to create additional facilities for cricket, archery, balloon as-

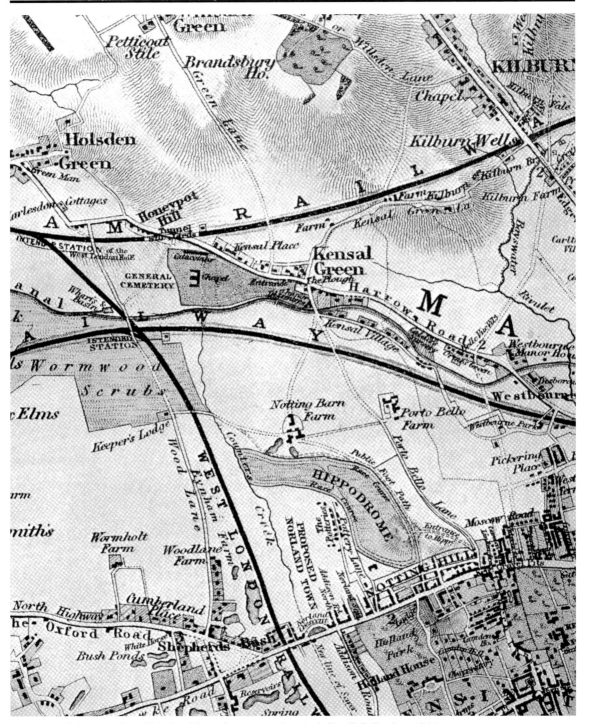

56. *Map of the area in which the Hippodrome was located. By E R Davies 1841.*

57. Notting Barn, near the racecourse, c.1830

58. Henry Rich, 1st Earl of Holland. From the oil painting by D. Mytens.

cents etc. The meeting of May 1839 was favoured by a "brilliant and immense assemblage of the nobility and gentry" and unblemished by the presence of even "a single drunken, riotous, disorderly or ill-behaved person or mendicant". Unfortunately for Whyte, though, the course's heavy clay soil proved unsuitable for racing and the land was attracting lively interest as a potential area for building. The last race at the Hippodrome was run on June 4th 1841.

David Hockney (1937-)

After studying at the Royal College of Art (1959-62) Hockney took a flat in Powis Terrace – 'cheap and large, meandering through two houses' – which became his main base until 1978. By 1967 he had already achieved a sufficiently iconic status to appear alongside Mick Jagger and Michael Caine in Peter Whitehead's *Tonite Let's All Make Love in London*. Hockney's celebrated double

portrait of fashion designer Ossie Clark and his wife, designer Celia Birtwell, was painted in 1970-71. Hockney's visitors in Powis Terrace included Sir John Gielgud, Cecil Beaton and W H Auden.[28]

Holland House

Originally built for Sir Walter Cope (*qv*) to the designs of John Thorpe, this property passed via Cope's wife to his daughter and sole heir, Isobel, and thus to her husband, Sir Henry Rich, ennobled as Earl of Holland in Lincolnshire in 1629, the year in which imposing gatepiers were added by Nicholas Stone, to the designs of Inigo Jones. Holland added a west wing (stood 1639-1704) and an over-sized range of stables (built 1638-40). Unfortunately Holland's political sense did not match either his looks or his fortune and being first for Parliament and then for the king in the civil wars, he ended up losing his head, a few weeks after his monarch did, in March 1649.

For a while the house became a headquarters for the formidable Col. Fairfax, Cromwell's son-in-law but it was returned to the family's possession and passed from Lady Holland to her son (died 1701), who also inherited the earldom of Warwick. His widow married Joseph Addison (*qv*). In 1721 the Holland title expired with the death of the fourth earl in his early twenties. The property then passed to the Edwardes family, created Barons Kensington in the 1770s. In 1746 the house was taken by Henry Fox, who became Baron Holland and bought the freehold in 1768. Fox's long political career with the Whig interest peaked with his appointment as Paymaster General, a position which enabled him to pocket the interest from public funds not actually in use, a particularly valuable perquisite during the Seven

59. *Holland House from the south. Painting by J. Vardy, 1752.*

society beauties and whose brilliant oratory won the admiration of the Commons. Fox spent almost his entire career in opposition but did move the bill to abolish the slave trade shortly before his death. The third Baron Holland (died 1840) and his beautiful but bossy wife Elizabeth (died 1845) made Holland House the most scintillating literary cultural rendezvous in London. They also continued to improve the house and grounds. (Lady Holland is credited with the importation of dahlias to England.) Their librarian, Buonauiti, is credited with laying out the Iris Garden (1812) and the Dutch (originally Portuguese) Garden (1812). Such expenditures necessitated the disposal of parcels of the grounds for building up as

Years War (1756-63) which had vastly increased military expenditures.

Henry Fox's son was Charles James Fox (1749-1806), the gambler and libertine, whose slovenly habits proved no barrier to the friendship of the Prince of Wales or the adoration of

60. *Holland House in 1789. Drawn by G Samuel.*

61. *Charles James Fox. After the painting by John Opie.*

it was still possible to shoot woodcock in the grounds of the house as late as 1905. Holland House remained in the Ilchester line for eighty years. The sixth Earl was something of a scholar, producing *Chronicles of Holland House* (1937) and *Home of the Hollands 1605-1820* (1937). Holland House enjoyed its last hours of glory in July 1939 when King George VI and Queen Elizabeth attended a ball there. The main building was severely damaged by incendiary bombs on September 27/28 1940. The remains were acquired by the London County Council in 1952. The former east wing of the house was remodelled (1955-7) by (Sir) Hugh Casson *(qv)* as the King George VI Memorial Youth Hostel, extended in 1990-1. The Ice House was converted (1975) to become an exhibition area, like the surviving Orangery and Conservatory converted from the stables of 1638-40. Also surviving are a colonnaded causeway of 1890 and the early nineteenth century stables.

Holland Park Estate

This horse-shoe shaped development, built between 1860 and 1879, was classy from the outset. Some of the houses had thirty rooms and the builders were pledged to spend at least £2,000 on each of them. The census of 1871 shows 30 occupied houses, with an average of thirteen occupants, half of them servants; other servants, such as coachmen and grooms lived in Holland Park Mews. Twelve households were headed by active or retired

residential areas such as Addison Road *(qv)*. The poor health of the fourth Lord Holland (died 1859) did little to diminish the role of Holland House as a glittering social centre and in 1849 he entertained Victoria and Albert to a 'Scottish fete' so successful it was repeated the next year. But this could only be sustained by selling off the land which became Holland Park *(qv)*. After he died childless Lord Holland's widow moved out but only to return periodically as hostess of further lavish entertainments. By 1873 her extravagant lifestyle and accumulated debts forced her to make the house over to her heir in another line of the Fox family, the fifth Earl of Ilchester (died 1905). The Earl continued the process of selling off the grounds for building areas such as Melbury Road *(qv)*, although

62. Elizabeth, Lady Holland. Painting by Fagan.

63. *A scene in the garden of Holland House.*

merchants and there were also three barristers, two clergymen, a peer, an Italian prince and the wealthy and cultured Ionides family *(qv)*. They would shortly be joined by MPs, a Lord Mayor, the Maharajah of Lahore and the engineer Sir William Fairbairn *(qv)*. No. 80 was replaced by Duke's Lodge in 1939. No. 1, home of the Ionides family was demolished following war damage, as was 1a.

Holland Park Community School

Holland Park was London's first purpose-built comprehensive school, opened in 1958. Its construction involved the demolition of Moray Lodge *(qv)* and Bedford Lodge *(qv)*, although Thorpe Lodge *(qv)* was pre-

64. *The Kyoto Garden was opened in 1991 by the Prince of Wales and the Crown Prince of Japan as part of the Japan Festival to mark the centenary of the Japan Society of Great Britain.*

served to become a Sixth Form Centre. Local sensitivities restricted the height of school buildings to four storeys. The school's reputation as an educational trendsetter was marked by the social mix of its intake, ranging from the children of Cabinet Ministers Tony Benn *(qv)* and Roy Jenkins *(qv)* to newly-arrived immigrants.

The school's landmark status enabled it to attract such high-profile visitors as Bill Gates and Nelson Mandela. It was also, perhaps, a natural setting for the gauche teacher played by Michael Crawford in the 1965 comedy *The Knack*. Heavily over-subscribed, it has 1,550 pupils from over a hundred nationalities; at the time of writing these include 300 refugees or asylum-seekers. Half the students receive free school meals and more than half also speak a language other than English. Few now come from the surrounding area. Kensington has only three other state secondary schools, all Roman Catholic.[29]

Herbert Hoover

When Herbert Clark Hoover (1874-1964), future 39th President of the United States, moved into Red House, Hornton Street in 1907, he was a respected mining engineer, with experience in the US, Australia and China. His lease still quaintly warned tenants against allowing their cattle to wander onto local highways. Hoover had just sold his partnership in a British mining company for £169,000 and in 1908 established his own London-based

65. *The Red House, Hornton Street, home of Herbert Hoover. View from the garden. A watercolour by M Conway, 1904.*

consulting firm to promote oil exploration. As the Royal Navy had just opted to switch from coal to oil Hoover's timing was impeccable. He soon had offices in New York, San Francisco, Paris and Petrograd. In 1909 he financed the authoritative *Mining Magazine* which hyped shares in companies he controlled. By 1910 Hoover was worth $3,000,000 but still living in the modest eight-room house with the large rose garden on Hornton Street, although he did also have a country house at Stratford-on-Avon as well. He had time for writing on game conservation and mining and, with his wife's assistance translated Agricola's classic metallurgical treatise *De Re Metallica* (1555). What brought Hoover to public prominence was the outbreak of war in 1914, which left 150,000 neutral Americans – visitors, students and a Wild West show touring Poland – stranded in Europe, many of whom had run out of funds.

As the head of a relief committee based in the Savoy Hotel, Hoover used his superb talent for administrative improvisation to finance, with cash put up by a consortium of American businessmen, the repatriation of 120,000 of his compatriots in six weeks. Of the $1,500,000 disbursed on trust less than $300 went unredeemed by borrowers. Hoover was asked to head the Commission for Relief in Belgium and later directed the scheme of voluntary rationing in the US. His brilliant direction of these ambitious and worthy projects raised his public profile and popularity to set him on his way to the White House. The site of Red House is now covered by Kensington Town Hall. In 1932 Hoover's portrait was painted by Philip de Laszlo *(qv)*.

Hornton Street Chapel

This Congregational chapel, built in 1794-5, stood at the junction of Hornton Street

54

and Hornton Place. The promoters included the piano maker John Broadwood and William Forsyth, gardener of Kensington Palace, for whom Forsythia is named. After the congregation moved to Horbury chapel it became a Baptist chapel in 1858 and was demolished c.1927. Its ministers included John Leifchild (1780-1862), minister from 1808 to 1824, who became a prolific author on religious topics; his successor Robert Vaughan (1795-1868) became a professor of history at University College, London; John Stoughton (1807-97), another historian, took over in 1843.

John Callcott Horsley

Horsley's father, William (1774-1858) was an organist and musician famous for composing glees. He married the daughter of the composer John Wall Callcott (qv), brother of Sir Augustus Wall Callcott (qv) and lived at 1 High Row, Kensington, where Mendelssohn was a frequent caller. John (1817-1903) was initially educated at a school which stood on the site now occupied by the Carmelite convent. His sister Mary married the engineer Isambard Kingdom Brunel who accompanied Horsley on a visit to Italy. The portrait John Horsley painted of his famous brother-in-law is now in the National Portrait Gallery. Apart from domestic and genre scenes Horsley also contributed frescoes (1842-8) to the new Houses of Parliament and in 1843 designed the world's first Christmas card at the suggestion of

Henry Cole, who would become the first director of the Victoria & Albert Museum. In 1858 Horsley commissioned the then unknown Richard Norman Shaw (qv) to repair his country house at Cranbrook in Kent. As Rector of the Royal Academy (1875-90) Horsley attracted ridicule by his opposition to paintings of the nude, becoming known as 'Clothes Horsley'. Horsley's friends included Millais, Leech, Holman Hunt, Mulready and Frith (qqv). Horsley's *Recollections of a Royal Academician* was published in the year of his death. He died at 1 High Row and was buried at Kensal Green. An extensive archive of Horsley family papers and photographs is now in the Bodleian Library.[30]

Hospitals

Apart from a small dispensary for out-patients, opened in Church Street in 1849, North Kensington had no hospital until the St Marylebone Poor Law Infirmary was built in St Charles Square in 1881. The design was based on five separated pavilions, a principle advocated by Florence Nightingale to limit cross-infection. The dominant central tower incorporated a chimney and water tanks. The hospital also had the benefit of its own Artesian well (qv). It changed its name to the St Charles Hospital in 1922. In 1896 the dispensary acquired an eleven-bed ward for children. In 1928 it was reaccommodated in St Quintin Avenue as the Princess Louise Hospital for Children. Ironically this eventually became a geriatric unit.

W H Hudson

William Henry Hudson (1841-1922) belatedly won acclaim for his evocation of the Argentinian pampas of his birth but passed nearly half his life in the less than wide open spaces afforded by 40 St Luke's Villas, Westbourne Park, where he lived from 1886 until his death. Hudson, the offspring of poor American immigrants of English descent, gained his education largely by running wild on the family ranch, acquiring a lifelong interest in natural history and in particular birds. Typhus, followed by rheumatic fever at 15, impaired his heart, blighting hopes of a frontier life, and turned him to writing. Arriving in London in 1874, Hudson passed decades in obscure poverty before gaining recognition with *The Naturalist in La Plata* (1892) and *British Birds* (1895). In 1901 he was awarded a civil list pension of £150 a year. His best known work, the novel *Green Mansions*, appeared in 1904 and, slowly over the next decade, made huge sales on both sides of the Atlantic, although he disparaged it privately. It was not Hudson that had changed but the public, as middle-class readers, immured in cities of ever-growing immensity and not yet liberated by the motor car, became eager for evocations of the wild and increasingly receptive to romances imbued with rural lore and folk wisdom. The support of Galsworthy (qv) and Foreign Secretary Sir Edward Grey, an amateur but eminent ornithologist, helped to ensure recognition of *Hudson's Adventures among Birds* (1913) and joyous memoir of boyhood, appropriately entitled *Far Away and Long Ago* (1918). Hudson's collected works run to twenty-five volumes. His memorial is a bird sanctuary, with decorative work by Jacob Epstein, in Hyde Park. Hudson named the Royal Society for the Protection of Birds as "high residuary legatee" of his estate.

Joseph Hume

Not to be confused with the famous radical MP of the same name, this Hume (1767-1843) was a Somerset House clerk with literary ambitions who produced a dire blank-verse version of Dante's *Inferno* and made his residence, Montpellier House, Notting Hill, a rendezvous for more talented figures such as Lamb, Hazlitt and Godwin. Hume was buried at Kensal Green.

William Holman Hunt

Holman Hunt (1827-1910) was perhaps the only founder member of the Pre-Raphaelite movement to remain unswervingly true to its principle of "truth in preference to beauty". His most famous painting is *The Light of the World* (1854), painted for Keble College, Oxford, though the version in St Paul's has been seen by far more people. Other well-known examples of Hunt's work include *The Hireling Shepherd* (1852), *The Awakening Conscience* (1853) and *The Scapegoat* (1856). Rich in detail, Hunt's works, nearly all reli-

66. *William Holman Hunt.*

gious or moralistic in subject-matter, look as though they took a long time to paint and they did. To deepen his understanding of the Bible and its setting he spent years in the Holy Land. Hunt lived at 1 Tor Villa, Campden Hill in 1857, No. 18 Melbury Road from 1903 until his death. The major product of those years was his autobiographical account *Pre-Raphaelitism and the Pre-Raphaelite Brotherhood* (1905).

Colin Hunter

Brought up on the coast of Scotland, Hunter (1841-1904) specialised in pictures of fisher-folk and seafaring, although he also produced water colours and etchings. Hunter's handsome home, Lugar, at 14 Melbury Road was built in 1876, damaged during World War Two and then demolished.

Sir William Oliphant Hutchison

After recovering from severe wounds received with the

67. *Holman Hunt's home in Melbury Road.*

artillery in France, in 1923 Hutchison (1889-1970) settled in Ladbroke Road, where he became close friends with a fellow Scot, James Pryde (qv). A successful portraitist, Hutchison was also a highly successful director of the Glasgow School of Art (1932-43), which was housed in buildings designed by another friend, Charles Rennie Mackintosh. Hutchison subsequently returned to work in Cheniston Gardens Studios. His portraits included the Queen, Ramsay MacDonald and Dorothy L Sayers and his lifelong friend and fellow Scot and portraitist Sir James Gunn.

Incomers

Given the rural character of North Kensington until the nineteenth century the label incomer might be applied to much of its subsequent population. The Irish figured significantly among the population of the Potteries (*qv*) and almost certainly accounted for many of the female servants of more affluent localities nearby. Scottish aristocrats featured prominently as tenants of Campden Hill mansions, as did Scots among the artistic community. An Indian (*qv*) student community can be dated from the late nineteenth century. A Jewish presence was registered by the establishment of local synagogues (*qv*). The 1930s witnessed the arrival of more Jews and refugees from the Spanish civil war. During World War Two inhabitants of Malta and Gibraltar were evacuated to temporary accommodation in the area. Writing about the war-time period Osbert Lancaster (*qv*) included Indian students, alongside 'Viennese professors' as typical residents of Notting Hill. He might have added Serbs (who took over St Clement's church to make it St Sava's), Ukrainians and Russians, who in 1955 established the Pushkin Club which meets at 46 Ladbroke Grove. Caribbean migrants in the 1950s became victims of Rachman (*qv*) and riots (*qv*) but established carnival (*qv*) as Notting Hill's most characteristic institution. Some, however, discovered that a street party for the 1977 Jubilee was not to include 'foreigners' – so they held their own. More Spanish, especially from Galicia, came in the 1960s, looking for work. Portuguese and Moroccans followed them in search of a better life, mostly working in hotels and catering. A Sikh gurdwara was built in Norland Road *c*.1965.

More recently Sudanese, Somalis, Eritreans and Ethiopians have sought asylum from war and oppressive regimes. Recovering the stories of the otherwise voiceless has become the mission of the Kensington and Chelsea Community History Group which was established in 1989.[31]

Indian Ink

The tutorial college established in Powis Square in the 1870s attracted so many aspiring candidates for the Indian Civil Service selection examinations that it spread into six houses. Many of the students were of mixed Anglo-Indian parentage. Billeted in nearby streets, they gained the area the nickname of 'Little India'. The proprietor of the college, Walter Wren (1834-98) became a Liberal MP.

Jawaharlal Nehru (1889-1964), first Prime Minister of independent India, lived at 60 Elgin Crescent in 1910 and 1912 while reading for the bar. His lawyer father intended him for the Indian Civil Service and had him educated at Harrow and Cambridge before deciding that the boy should switch to the law. Nehru was enrolled in Middle Temple, qualified in 1912 but found his vocation in the movement for Indian independence, spending many of his adult years in prisons rather than in the courts. Nehru's deputy as Prime Minister, Sardar Vallabhbhai Javerbai Patel (1875-1950), lived at 23 Aldridge Road Villas, entered Middle Temple and was

called to the bar a year after Nehru. Both men, despite their passionate adherence to the cause of Indian independence, retained a predilection for the restrained dandyism characteristic of an English barrister.

Indian poet, biographer, anthologist and TV documentary-maker Dom Moraes (1938-) once lived in the same Notting Hill house as John Heath-Stubbs and John Gawsworth. At the age of twenty Moraes became the youngest, and first non-English, person to win the Hawthornden Prize. His three volumes of memoirs were republished as *A Variety of Absences* (2003).

Jean Ingelow

A poet and writer of children's stories, Ingelow (1820-97) lived at 15 Holland Street (1855-75) where Ingelow House now stands. Born in Boston, Lincs., she found a champion in Tennyson, a Lincolnshire man, who once said "you do the trick better than I do." It was a good job she could write because after her family's bank failed she had to rely on herself to support her mother and two brothers. They seem to have been less than understanding of their collective predicament because Ingelow had to rent rooms in a house opposite to have peace and quiet for writing. (But she seems to have had a philosophic disposition, once observing that "worry is interest paid on trouble before it falls due".) Ingelow's friends included Ruskin, the widowed Browning and Christina Rossetti. Her most celebrated poem, inspired by a terrible flood disaster, was *The High Tide on the Coast of Lincolnshire 1571*, published in her *Poems* of 1863 which sold thirty editions, the last one in 1921. Published in America in 1875 she sold 200,000 copies there, which may not have done her any good as the USA had not acknowledged international copyright conventions then. On the other hand an American ship was named after her and when Tennyson died in 1892 American writers petitioned Queen Victoria to appoint Ingelow his successor as Laureate. She is memorialized by a brass tablet in St Barnabas *(qv)* and was buried in Brompton cemetery.

Ionides family

Constantine Ipliktzis settled in England in 1815 with a view to exporting Manchester textiles to Greece and Turkey. His son Alexander Constantine (1810-90) changed his name to Ionides in homage to Ion, mythical ancestor of the Greeks, began collecting art and in 1864 acquired 1 Holland Park. His sons Alexander Alexander Ionides ('Alecco') (1840-98) and Constantine Alexander Ionides (1833-1900) carried on the tradition of collecting and patronage. Watts *(qv)* painted some twenty portraits of members of the Ionides family. Jacques Dalou made a bust of Miss Helen Ionides as a child, which is now in the Victoria & Albert Museum. Other artistic protégés of the Ionides included Burne-

Jones, Rossetti and Whistler. Legros acted as Constantine Ionides' artistic adviser. Alecco spent £2,361 having his house, 8 Holland Villas Road, decorated by William Morris. Included in the commission was a tapestry, *The Forest*, and a large hand-tufted carpet, the originals of which are now in the V & A. (The carpet pattern, known as Carbrook, is now available in kit form for needlepoint fans.) Philip Webb and Walter Crane *(qv)* also worked on 1 Holland Park and Webb designed an extension for 8 Holland Villas Road. The architect Thomas Jeckyll designed a wing for 1 Holland Park which included a master bedroom and "an Anglo-Japanese billiard room".

Alexander Constantine Ionides' daughter Aglaia Ionides Coronio (1834-1906) became Morris's confidante and pupil. Constantine Alexander Ionides' collection of 1,138 pictures, prints and drawings, ranging from Botticelli and Rembrandt to Corot and Degas, was left to the V & A.

Roy Harris Jenkins, Baron Jenkins of Hillhead

The youngest MP in the Commons when he was elected for Labour in 1948, Roy Jenkins (1920-2003) served as Home Secretary and Chancellor of the Exchequer, before becoming President of the European Commission. A founder-member of the breakaway Social Democratic Party, he served as its first leader in 1982-83. In 1987 he

moved to the Lords and was also elected to the highly congenial post of Chancellor of the University of Oxford. Renowned as a *bon viveur*, Jenkins was also a highly accomplished biographer, producing acclaimed revaluations of Dilke, Asquith, Gladstone and Churchill. Roy Jenkins lived at 33 Ladbroke Square (1964-80) and then at 2 Kensington Park Gardens until shortly before his death, when he moved into Hereford Mansions.

Claudia Jones

Born in Trinidad but raised in Harlem, Communist activist and journalist Claudia Jones (1915-64) was imprisoned four times before McCarthyite harassment led to her deportation. Much to the relief of the Trinidadian government she chose to settle in Britain, where she became the founding editor of the *West Indian Gazette*. Jones took an active role in promoting carnival *(qv)* and seeking punishment for the murderers of Kelso Cochrane *(qv)*. Dying of a stroke in her sleep, she is buried next to Karl Marx in Highgate cemetery. The Claudia Jones Organisation, an Afro-Caribbean women's support organisation based in Stoke Newington, has planted a garden in her memory.[32]

Kensal Green Cemetery

Britain's second census, taken in 1811, showed that London's population had passed the million mark. In the 1820s alone it increased by a stag-

68. *The proposed design for Kensal Green Cemetery, c.1832.*

gering 20%. More living meant more dead. The pressure on already overcrowded churchyards (some containing 3,000 burials per acre) created a crisis of corruption – physical as well as financial. In 1824, impressed by the example of Père Lachaise cemetery (established in 1804) in Paris, the barrister George Carden (1789-1874) began to plan the establishment of a similar enterprise (originally intended for Primrose Hill) which would bring new standards of design, hygiene and management to the task of disposing of the capital's corpses. This led in 1830 to the establishment of the General Cemetery Company. Britain's first experience of the terrors and horror of a cholera epidemic in 1831-2 added a further urgency to the enterprise, for two reasons. Firstly, it

created ten thousand extra deaths in the capital alone. Secondly, the nature of the new disease was misunderstood by the medical profession and blamed on 'miasma' – bad air – allegedly produced by foul churchyards. Relocating burial grounds away from the centre of the metropolis to airy heights, where corrupting odours would be rapidly dispersed, was therefore deemed highly desirable. The petition placed before Parliament by Andrew Spottiswoode MP, a friend of Carden's, begged for "the removal of the metropolitan graveyards to places where they would be less prejudicial to the health of the inhabitants." Kensal Green, 150 feet above sea-level, became the first of new burying grounds at Brompton, Highgate, Nunhead, Tower Hamlets etc. over the course of

the following decade. Finance for the Kensal Green project was put up by Sir John Dean Paul (died 1852), a governor of the Bank of England. The first tranche of £9,500 was used to purchase a site of fifty-five acres, to which a further twenty-two acres were to be added in the 1860s. The competition to design the lay-out and buildings of the cemetery was won by H E Kendall (1776-1875), who submitted a scheme in the newly fashionable Gothic mode, including the truly Arthurian touch of a watergate entrance from the Grand Junction Canal *(qv)*. Sir John Dean Paul, however, was adamant for the (more transiently fashionable) 'Greek revival' style, so the commission went to his favoured protégé, John Griffith (1796-1888) of Finsbury, who

69. The entrance to the Cemetery, c.1845.

70. Inside the Cemetery c.1845.

71. The tomb of William Mulready, designed by Godfrey Sykes.

had been one of the judges. (Kendall must have been a philosophical loser as he ended up being buried in his rival's creation). The first section of burying-ground was consecrated for use by the Bishop of London in 1833 and the initial phase of construction largely completed by 1837. Not only did the cemetery offer a choice of Anglican (Doric) and Nonconformist (Ionic) chapels, it also had a colonnade and state-of-the-art technology in the form of a hydraulic lift to serve its catacombs. Consumer choice was a paramount concern, with grieving relatives offered the choice of catacomb, mausoleum, bricklined vault or traditional earth grave. Plots were granted on a perpetual freehold. The grounds were landscaped with eight hundred specimen trees. Although the share price advanced satisfactorily from £30 to £52, the flow of business was relatively modest – some 18,000 interments in the first nineteen years of use. What turned the corner was the burial in 1843 of a member of the royal family, Augustus Frederick, Duke of Sussex (1773-1843), sixth son of George III, who had been appalled at the shambles attending the burial of King William IV and specifically chose Kensal Green over Windsor. Many of the more elaborate early tombs were made of expensively imported Carrara marble, which proved an unwise choice, given the corrosive proximity of the nearby gasworks. Improved railways made Scottish granites accessible in the later nineteenth century and these were to prove much more durable.

Kensal Green cemetery became a Victorian Valhalla and now houses the graves of some eight hundred worthies thought sufficiently eminent to merit an entry in the *Dictionary of National Biography*, including its first editor, Sir Leslie Stephen, the father of Virginia Woolf. Others buried there who are treated elsewhere in this book include architect Thomas Allom, painters Sir A W Callcott, William

72. *The Cemetery Chapel. The tomb of the Duke of Sussex in the right mid-ground is flanked by short stone columns.*

74. *Monument to radical Robert Owen.*

73. *The tomb of the Gatti family, owners of restaurants and ice wells. This is in St Mary's RC cemetery.*

75. *Monument to tightrope walker, Emile Blondin.*

Mulready, J H Pollen, Thomas Rowbotham, Alfred Clint and W P Frith, illustrator John Leech and cartoonist Phil May, novelist Harrison Ainsworth, the Irish agitator Feargus O'Connor, actress Madame Vestris, explorer John McDouall Stuart, businessman William Whiteley and fashion designer Ossie Clark. Freddie Mercury of Queen, sometime occupant of 12 Stafford Terrace, was cremated at Kensal Green but his ashes were taken thence to be scattered at Mumbai (Bombay). Further significant graves include those of the

76. Monument to Belgian Soldiers who died in the First World War.

architects Philip Hardwick and Decimus Burton; artists Daniel Maclise, George Cruikshank and Owen Jones; writers Thomas Hood, Leigh Hunt, Wilkie Collins, W M Thackeray, Henry Mayhew and Anthony Trollope; publishers John Cassell and John Murray; dramatist Terence Rattigan, whose ashes were brought from the Caribbean to be interred in the family vault; pioneer of computing Charles Babbage; George Birkbeck, creator of Mechanics' Institutes; engineers Isambard Kingdom Brunel and his father Sir Marc Brunel and Sir Joseph Bazalgette, mastermind of London's sewerage system; Sir William Siemens, inventor of the blast furnace; doctor Richard ('Bright's disease') Bright and Thomas Wakley, founder of *The Lancet*; and stage stars William Charles Macready, Charles Kemble, Fanny Kemble, Michael William ("I dreamt that I dwelt in marble

halls") Balfe. Among those who defy such general categorisation are tight-rope superstar Emile Blondin (Jean Francois Gravelet), who once cooked an omelette half-way across Niagara Falls; the wit and preacher the Revd Sydney Smith; garden designer J C Loudon; celebrity chef Alexis Soyer; Andrew Ducrow, trick-rider and circus owner, who, at a cost of £3,000 designed his own tomb – "erected by genius for the reception of its remains" (dismissed by *The Builder* as 'ponderous coxcombry'); and purveyor of patent medicines John St John Long, who was twice acquitted of manslaughter and died at 36, refusing himself to take his own alleged cure for consumption; Sir Anthony Panizzi, librarian of the British Museum and creator of its great Reading Room; *the* W H Smith and Major W C Wingfield, inventor of lawn tennis. In St Mary's Cemetery,

opened in 1858, adjacent (but actually outside the borough boundary) are buried the celebrated Crimean nurse Mary Seacole; Cardinals Wiseman and Manning *(qv)*; financier Sir Ernest Cassell; conductor Sir John Barbirolli and pioneer television interviewer Gilbert Harding – and, in the first eight years of its existence, 12,500 unfamed Irish who fled the Great Hunger of the 1840s to find work in London. Apart from the dead there are also the living. The cemetery functions as a nature reserve, supporting foxes and half the species of butterfly found in Britain. It is still run by the General Cemetery Company and is the largest in Britain in private ownership. The Friends of Kensal Green Cemetery were formed in 1990 and have achieved the full restoration of the Dissenters' chapel.[33]

Kensal New Town

In the fourteenth century the area was known as Kingsholt (holt = wood), which became corrupted as Kingshall, then Kinshall, Kensall and finally Kensal.

Mostly rough grazing when it supplied firewood to Westminster Abbey and yielded acorns to fatten the monks' herds of swine, the area passed to Henry VIII and then to his last wife Catherine Parr. By the nineteenth century most of the area was in the possession of the Jenkins and Talbot families. The talented but alcoholic painter George Morland (1763-1804) was a regular frequenter of the Plough Inn here. Novelist Harrison Ainsworth *(qv)* was

77. *A row of cottages in East Row, Kensal Town. Watercolour by W E Kell, 1911.*

78. *The Plough, a well-known pub at Kensal Green, patronised by the artist, George Morland. Drawing by Mary and Robert Banks.*

a local resident. The area was developed by absentee Welsh lawyer William Kinnaird Jenkins on four fields on which he initially built four terraces of cottages between 1841 and 1851. By that date the population had reached 2,344, of whom only 16% were over 45 and 41% were under sixteen. A similar percentage came from beyond the Home Counties. By 1860 the new community had acquired a Wesleyan chapel and seven pubs. Bounded by the Grand Junction Canal *(qv)*, the Great Western Railway and the Western Gas Company, the insalubrious locality attracted the impoverished Irish, many of whom lived by keeping pigs, or relying on the earnings of wives doing laundry for the residents of the more affluent districts to the south. A second phase of building from the 1860s (when the population increased by over a third) was completed by the 1880s and mostly accommodated workers at the gasworks or on the railway.

The churches of St Andrew and St Philip (1870), Our Lady of the Holy Souls (1882) and St Thomas (1889) were built to meet the spiritual needs of the community. In 1873 what has been claimed as the first crèche in the country was started in Edenham Street. The number of laundries continued to grow, reaching 57 by 1896, 41 of them in South Row. Retailing employed a fifth of the local male population. Hiring out horses for omnibuses, charabancs, dust-carts and delivery and removal vans was another prominent local trade. Other local employers included Sanderson's paint factory, Askey's, who made ice-cream wafers, and three dairy depots.

The fact that the area was technically part of Chelsea, before local government reorganisation in 1899, ensured its continued neglect until Kensington was reluctantly obliged to take it in. Booth classified over 55% of the inhabitants ("ill-fed, ragged, hatless and unwashed") as living in poverty, the area exhibiting "most of the features which, combined, lead to poverty and low life: canal and railway, gas works, isolation and the washing industry".

In 1911 Emslie J. Horniman presented an acre of ground to serve as a much-needed park. In 1928-9 the common lodging-house for men in Kensal Road was converted into a women's refuge by the sister-in-law of G K Chesterton (*qv*). Slum clearance schemes eradicated hundreds of basement dwellings in the 1930s. In the 1950s and 1960s the area between Golborne Road and Bosworth Road was redeveloped to the designs of Lord Holford, the area to the east being redeveloped around Trellick Tower (*qv*). Not before time. The 1968 Notting Hill Housing Survey revealed that at 232 per acre the population density of the Golborne area was the highest in England and Wales and that 80% of residents had to share such basic amenities as kitchen, bathroom or lavatory. Social innovation was represented by the opening of Britain's first Adventure Playground (1960), Law Centre (1970) and Neighbourhood Council (1971). Of the 2,300 buildings erected during the Victorian period only some 300 remain, the oldest being the former Middle Row Chapel of 1852, now a music studio.[34]

Kensington News

The *Kensington Gazette*, initially a free four-page 12" x 9" effort supported by advertising revenue was produced by local printer Charles James Strutt. The paper expanded to bear a cover price of a penny but Strutt's departure ended the venture after two years. In 1865 printer James Wakeham (died 1885) began publishing the *Kensington and Chelsea News* which became the *Kensington News and West London Times* in 1869. The newspaper was the first to expose the sleazy world of slum landlord Rachman (*qv*)

79. *A slum in Kensal Road, in 1967.*

80. *The offices of the Kensington News decorated for the Queen's jubilee in 1897.*

in the 1950s.

It also sponsored the 'Brighter Kensington and Chelsea' garden scheme as the district struggled to throw off its legacy of wartime neglect. The *Kensington News* was acquired by North West London Press in 1965 and merged with half a dozen other west London papers when it became part of the London Newspaper Group in 1972. Past employees of the *Kensington News* include film critic Barry Norman and writer Gavin Weightman.

Kensington Park Gardens

Politician and biographer Roy Jenkins lived at No. 2, scientist Sir William Crookes at No. 7 and adventurer Col. Richard Meinertzhagen at No. 17 (*qqv*). No. 24 is home to the London programme of Syracuse University (*qv*) and was originally the home of C H Blake, developer of the Ladbroke Estate (*qv*). No. 31 was home to Arthur and Sylvia Llewelyn-Davies, the Darling family in J M Barrie's *Peter Pan*. Sylvia was the daughter of the *Punch* cartoonist and novelist George du Maurier, author of *Trilby* and thus the sister of the actor Gerald du Maurier, the first Captain Hook and father of author Daphne du Maurier.

Kensington Temple

Built in 1848-9 to accommodate the Congregationalist worshippers of Hornton Street chapel (*qv*), it became the Kensington Temple, Church of the Foursquare Gospel in 1935. The adjacent Sunday school became the

81. *The Kensington Temple, 2004.*

Mercury Theatre (*qv*). Now Kensington Temple, Elim Pentecostal Church, the Temple is Elim's largest church. Founded in 1915 by Welsh preacher George Jeffreys, Elim has 600 churches in the UK and 9,000 worldwide.[35]

Louis (Lajos) Kossuth

Following the overthrow of the short-lived government of independent Hungary, of which he was briefly dictator in 1849, Kossuth (1802-94) (pronounced Ko-shoot) lived at 39 Chepstow Villas before moving on to the USA and finally settling in Turin. Lajos Kossuth University in Debrecen, Hungary is named in honour of 'The Father of Hungarian Democracy'.

Ladbroke Estate

Sir Robert Ladbroke was a banker, MP and Lord Mayor of London in 1747. In the 1750s his brother Richard bought four parcels of land

82. *Louis Kossuth.*

to the north of the 'Uxbridge Road'. His heir, Richard Weller, who took the surname Ladbroke as a condition of inheritance, began the development of the land for building, employing Thomas Allason (*qv*) as surveyor. An Act of Parliament of 1821 empowered Ladbroke to grant 99-year leases. Construction was, however, substantially delayed by the financial crisis of 1825 and the abortive experiment of the Hippodrome (*qv*) racecourse. The major phase of development began in the 1840s under James Weller Ladbroke (died 1847), the main promoters being Richard Roy, a solicitor, Charles Henry Blake (1794-1872), a former Calcutta merchant and director of the Hammersmith & City Railway, and the well-intentioned but ill-fated Dr Samuel Walker (*see p.9*). Allason's notion of a large circus bisected by a major thoroughfare may well have been derived from the unfulfilled 'British Circus' proposed by John Shaw (1776-1832) for the Eyre estate at St John's Wood, while the detached

83. Ladbroke Grove, 1866.

and semi-detached villas he envisaged may have derived from John Nash's Park Village on the edge of Regent's Park. The modest stucco-fronted designs of Robert Cantwell in Ladbroke Terrace resemble examples erected in Cheltenham where developer Richard Roy had a house built. Indeed, the street-names Ladbroke and Montpellier occur in both locations. Architectural historian Professor James Stevens Curl has suggested that the design of the communal gardens was based on ideas first advanced in 1835 by T Rutger, a correspondent of John Claudius Loudon's *The Gardener's Magazine*. In 1853 the bank rate suddenly rose from 2% to 5%, severely embarrassing many speculative builders and causing many ambitious residences to stand as half-completed shells until the following decade.[36]

Ladbroke Square Gardens

Designed by Thomas Allason *(qv)* and listed Grade II, this is London's second largest private communal garden, stretching over seven acres and laid out in 1849. Within survives a remnant of the entrance to the Hippodrome racecourse *(qv)*. During World War Two the tennis courts were dug up for allotments. In *The Information* (1995) Martin Amis christens the gardens 'Dogshit Park'.

Sir Osbert Lancaster

Born at No. 79 Elgin Crescent when it was "the very Acropolis of Edwardian propriety", Lancaster (1908-86) in his first volume of memoirs, *All Done from Memory* (1963), drew a vivid picture of its decayed state when he revisited it during World War Two – "all peeling paint and crumbling volutes", with the sub-division of grand family residences into cramped flats signified by the variety of their grimy net curtains and housing refugees "like the dark-age troglodytes who sheltered in the galleries and boxes of the Colosseum". These were a far cry from the residents of his youth – an actor, an authoress, Japanese diplomats and a youthful Nehru *(qv)*. Lancaster himself became a national institution after joining the *Daily Express* as a cartoonist in 1939. The domestic dilemmas and pronouncements of his creation, Maudie Littlehampton, for generations provided a knowing commentary on the changing mores of the English middle-classes. Lancaster, however, had several more strings to his bow and was an accomplished designer of stage sets and a humorous but incisive writer on architecture.

Lansdowne House

Built in 1900-4 as an artists' colony, at the expense of Sir Edmund Davis *(qv)* and to the designs of William Flockhart, Lansdowne House is dismissed by Pevsner as "incongruous in both scale and style". The original building, now 80 Lansdowne Road, had six apartments, each with a north-lit two-storey studio. Occupants shared communal bathrooms in the basement and had the use of a Real Tennis court. Residents have included Charles Shannon, Charles Ricketts, Glyn Philpot, F Cayley Robinson and James Pryde *(qqv)*. Converted to a suite of recording studios, Lansdowne House has been the venue for creating the notorious 1976 Sex Pistols *Anarchy* in the UK, the soundtracks of *Lord of the Rings, Captain Corelli's Mandolin* and *Billy Elliot* and the music for TV series such as *Band of Brothers* and *The Forsyte Saga*.[37]

Lao She (1899-1966)

China's most celebrated twentieth century author lived at 31 St James's Gardens from 1925 until 1928; an English Heritage blue plaque was unveiled there in 2003. A teacher, then known as Colin C Shu, at the then School of Oriental Studies of the University of London, Lao She (the pen name of Shi Qingchun) was an admirer of Fielding, Dickens and Hardy. He wrote about his own London experiences and also translated an erotic classic, *The Golden Lotus*. Returning to China in 1931, he wrote patriotic anti-Japanese propaganda. His *Rickshaw Boy* (1945) became a bestseller in English. A stage play, *Teahouse*, traced forty years of China's troubled modern history in the setting of a Beijing teahouse. Eleven of his works have been filmed and his epic saga *Four Generations* (English version *The Yellow Storm* 1951) became a TV mini-series. Honoured until the Cultural Revolution he committed suicide as a result of Red Guard persecution.[38]

Philip de Laszlo

Born Fulep Elek von Laszlo (1869-1937) in Pest, the son of a tailor, he was initially apprenticed to a photographer before studying art in Munich and Paris and establishing his reputation as a portraitist by painting Balkan royalty. In 1900 de Laszlo married Lucy Guinness, whom he had met in Munich. Arriving in London in 1907, the very year in which John

84. John Leech.

Singer Sargent renounced portraiture for landscape, he had another immense stroke of fortune when Edward VII saw his work and immediately commissioned a portrait of his daughter, Princess Victoria. Restyled as Philip Alexius Laszlo de Lambos, the artist was naturalized in 1914 but still interned in Holloway in 1917 for writing letters to his family. Cleared in 1919 he swiftly resumed a career which was to embrace 2,700 sitters, including four American presidents, two Popes, two Archbishops of Canterbury, Mussolini and Lloyd George (twice). The National Portrait Gallery holds more than a dozen of de Laszlo's portraits including those of Fildes (*qv*) and Henschel (*qv*), who would have been near neighbours when he took over West House from George Boughton (*qv*). The artist was himself sketched by David Low (*qv*). De Laszlo was honoured in his lifetime with twenty-two orders and seventeen medals but it was not until 2004, as

part of the Magyar Magic celebrations to mark Hungary's accession to the European Union, that the first ever retrospective of his work was organised, by Christie's, with the appropriate title *A Brush with Grandeur*.

John Leech

Leech's potential was spotted by the sculptor John Flaxman when Leech (1817-64) was just three. Flaxman advised against any formal instruction in drawing, trusting to the child's natural talent. In the event Leech was set to train as a doctor until his father's fortunes failed and he turned to art, immediately making his name with an adroit parody of the postal envelope designed by William Mulready (*qv*). In 1841, three weeks after the journal was founded, Leech joined *Punch*. The connection remained lifelong, Leech contributing some three thousand illustrations and receiving some £40,000 in return. Leech lived for some years at 62 Holland Park Road (then 31 Notting Hill Terrace). The extraordinary regard in which Leech continued to be held was marked by the two volume biography published by his friend W P Frith (*qv*) in 1891 and the London County Council's decision to honour his Thames-side birth-place with a plaque in 1907.

Frederic, Lord Leighton

The first painter to be ennobled (on his death bed), Leighton (1830-96) gained valuable publicity early in his career when, in 1855, Queen

85. *Lord Leighton. Caricature from Vanity Fair, 1872.*

Victoria bought his painting of *Cimabue's Madonna carried in Procession through the Streets of Florence* for £600. John Ruskin, the foremost critic of the century, praised the work as "very important and very beautiful". A peripatetic childhood had made Leighton fluent in four languages and brought him the friendship of writer George Sand and actress Fanny Kemble and of Thackeray (who prophesied – correctly – to Millais that Leighton would become President of the Royal Academy before Millais did). Leighton had fine features, a good tenor voice and a (selective) willingness to please, which led the artist George du Maurier to judge him "one of the world's little darlings, who won't make themselves agreeable to anything under a duchess." Leighton's subject-matter as a painter was often drawn from classical antiquity and, to a lesser extent, the East. His other projects included Elizabeth Barrett Browning's tomb, a series of frescoes in the Victoria and albert Museum and a mural for the Royal Exchange. Elected ARA in 1864, in 1866 he built the handsome residence at 12 Holland Park Road, now known as Leighton House *(qv)*. In 1869 he was elected RA and in 1878 PRA, a position for which his polished social skills most eminently fitted him. Leighton was also a keen member of the volunteer movement and served as colonel of the Artists' Rifles. One of Leighton's obituarists judged him to have been better at drapery than anatomy, more proficient in design than draughtsmanship, "often as nearly great as a man without creative genius can be." Leighton was buried in St Paul's. He never married. After his death the Leighton Fund was set up to purchase and commission works of art for public places.[39]

Leighton House

As much an art-gallery as a house – it has only one bedroom (except, of course, for servants' accommodation) – Leighton House was designed by the artist in collaboration with his 'old friend' George Aitchison RA. Aitchison would become Professor of Architecture at the Royal Academy (1887-1905) and President of the Royal Institute of British Architects (1896-9). Leighton's contribution, however, was no formality as he was to receive the RIBA's gold medal for the knowledge of architecture demonstrated in the background of his paintings. Planned in 1864 and completed by 1866, the first phase cost £4,500, for which one could have built a modest-sized parish church. In Pevsner's words the "reticent exterior conceals the most sumptuous and colourful nineteenth-century artist's house in London". Leighton continued to embellish and enlarge the building until his death thirty years later, adding a library and a second studio. The main studio, facing onto the garden, is over fifty feet long, decorated with a cast from the Parthenon frieze and has separate back stairs access for discreet use by models and dealers. The 13th to 17th century tiles, Cairene woodwork and Syrian glass for the fabulous Arab Hall (1877-9) were collected during a tour of the Middle East in 1873. Crane *(qv)* contributed a mosaic in the Persian mode. The alabaster capitals were carved by Sir Joseph Boehm from designs by the children's illustrator Randolph Caldecott. The design was inspired by the palace of La Zisa in Palermo. Apart from Leighton's own paintings the house contains works by Watts *(qv)*, Burne-Jones and Millais and tiles by de Morgan. The then Kensington Borough Council acquired the freehold in 1926, the Perrin Gallery being added by Halsey Ricardo *(qv)*.[40]

86. The Arab Hall at Leighton House.

Prue Leith

Prue Leith (1940-) studied at the Sorbonne and trained at the Cordon Bleu cookery school in London before starting her own outside catering service from her bedsitter in 1960. When she sold it in 1993 the business had a turnover of £13,000,000 and 300 staff. She started her restaurant, Leith's at 92 Kensington Park Road in 1969; it won a Michelin star in 1994. Leith's School of Food and Wine opened in 1975; there is a sister school in South Africa. Prue Leith subsequently became Chair of the British Food Trust, Chairman of the Royal Society of Arts, cookery editor of *The Guardian*, a director of British Rail, Safeway, Whitbread and the Halifax and was voted Businesswoman of the Year. Apart from her cookery books (*Cooking for Friends, The Well-Fed Baby, Entertaining with Style, Leith's Guide to Wine, Leith's Cookery Bible*) she has also published two novels.

Percy Wyndham Lewis

Born on his American father's yacht off the coast of Canada and educated at Rugby and the Slade, Lewis (1882-1957) led the life of a wandering artist in his twenties, dabbling in far right French politics before returning to England and being taken up by Ford Madox Ford (*qv*) and Ezra Pound (*qv*). Inventing his own rebel art movement, Vorticism, he almost immediately rejected it ('Art behaving as if it were politics') and became an official war artist. His inter-war years were marked by poverty, ill-

87. *Prue Leith's former restaurant in Kensington Park Road.*

ness, restless travel, the publication of twenty books and a flirtation with Nazism. Lewis spent the war in self-imposed North American exile, then returned to live at 27a Notting Hill Gate, a bomb-damaged flat which he used to epitomise the seedy condition of post-war Britain in his novel *Rotting Hill* (1951). Despite his track-record Lewis was soon rehabilitated – art critic of *The Listener*, Civil List pension, honorary Litt. D. from Leeds, Tate retrospective etc. Failing eyesight, however, blighted the closing years of his life, passed at 29 Notting Hill Studios. Hemingway said Lewis had the eyes of an unsuccessful rapist.[41]

Libraries

Perhaps it was the existence of well-stocked private libraries like those of Lord Macaulay (*qv*) or the household of G K Chesterton (*qv*) which delayed the advent of adequate public provision in such an affluent area as Ken-

sington. The penny-pinching vestry declined for so long to take advantage of legislation empowering parishes with over 10,000 inhabitants to raise a library rate of a half-penny in the pound that it was left to a local resident, James Haywood MP, to take the initiative in financing one, housed in a former shop at 106 Notting Hill Gate. The Vestry finally relented to take this into the public domain in 1887. Assistant librarian Herbert Jones became the first in the metropolis to begin building up a collection relating to the locality's history and topography. A North Kensington branch, opened in Ladbroke Grove in 1901, was the borough's first purpose-built library and the only one of the early buildings still in use. A children's service was inaugurated in 1912 but not until 1926 were borrowers allowed direct access to the shelves, rather than requesting titles selected from the catalogue. The Pembridge Square branch

88. *The library in Ladbroke Grove, c.1905.*

library was opened in 1955 to replace the post-war improvisation housed in a former surface air-raid shelter in Bulmer Mews. Kensington Library in Phillimore Walk was opened in 1960. The conservative designs of E Vincent Harris (which he described as 'a modern English Renaissance style ... manly ... dignified') provoked protest marches by art and architecture students.[42]

Linden Gardens

Known originally as Linden Grove (until 1877) and once protected by ornamental gates, this cul-de-sac was the first of James Ladbroke's plots to be developed. The largest of the early houses built there, with its own lake,

two acres of grounds, stables and a gardener's cottage was Linden Lodge, designed in 1826 by Thomas Allason (*qv*), who lived in it until 1838-9. (It was to be swept away within less than half a century to make way for the railway).

Royal Academician William Mulready (1786-1863), designer of the penny postage envelope depicting Britannia (famously caricatured for *Punch* by John Leech (*qv*)), lived at Kensington Gravel Pits from 1811 to 1827 and then at Linden Grove from 1828 until his death. Mulready's prodigious effort enabled him to graduate from illustrating children's books to humorous and sentimental genre painting. At seventy-five he was still self-critical

enough to attend "a little life school held by the painters in the neighbourhood of Kensington" to practise sketching at speed.

Landscape painter and book illustrator Thomas Creswick RA (1811-69) enjoyed unspectacular success and lived at 42 Linden Gardens [1838-66] and then occupied Mulready's house (now demolished) until his death. The advent of the Metropolitan Railway in 1864-8 prompted the redevelopment of the five acre estate between 1871 and 1878. In 1910, at the height of the Suffragette agitation, Sylvia Pankhurst was living at Mulready's old address. Dame Ivy Compton-Burnett (1884-1969), novelist of dysfunctional family life, lived at

71

89. John Linnell.

90. Little Campden House, built c.1690 to accommodate Princess (later Queen) Anne's suite when she and Prince George of Denmark were renting Campden House.

No. 97. Linden Gardens was also home to fashion designer Ossie Clark (1942-96) when living with his wife Celia Birtwell. Clark later moved to Cambridge Gardens and at the time of his murder by his lover in 1996 was living in Penzance Terrace. No. 49 Linden Gardens is the headquarters of several organisations representing Britain's Ukrainian community.

John Linnell

While still a child Linnell (1792-1882) was set to copying the genre paintings of George Morland even before becoming a pupil of landscape artist John Varley, who was also teaching the Irish artist William Mulready *(qv)*. Linnell entered the RA school when only thirteeen and won medals for life drawing and life modelling. From 1808 to 1811 he shared lodgings with Mulready at Kensington Gravel Pits *(qv)* and made a number of detailed local studies on walks in the area, including an oil painting of men working the pits to supply the London building trade.

This was acquired by the Tate Gallery in 1947. Linnell had known the locality since childhood because he regularly visited a cousin who was married to "a respectable farmer who lived on ... Portobello Lane ... and it is with this place that my pleasantest recollections are connected." Mulready would later move to Linden Gardens *(qv)*.

Linnell's first (1813) Royal Academy exhibit *Bird Catching*, was later retitled *Kensington 1814*. His pupils included Mary Shelley. In 1829 Linnell had a family home built at 38 Porchester Terrace, Bayswater and made portraits of some of the workmen in part payment of their wages. He enjoyed great success as a portraitist, with Peel, Malthus and Carlyle among his subjects, before changing to landscapes and retiring to Surrey in 1852. Linnell was William Blake's last patron and a supporter of the Pre-Raphaelites. Samuel Palmer became his son-in-law.[43]

Little Campden House

In 1850 this building was divided into two dwellings, the eastern part also known as The Elms (later 30 Gloucester Walk) and the western as Lancaster Lodge (later 80 Hornton Street). Around 1853 genre painter Augustus Egg (1816-63) moved into The Elms. In 1869 William Morris's friend Philip Webb built a studio in the garden of Lancaster Lodge for the genre painter R B Martineau (1826-69), a pupil of Holman Hunt *(qv)* but Martineau died before it was even completed. In the 1870s the eastern part was the home of actor Alfred Wigan and his wife. George Vicat Cole *(qv)* lived in the house after 1874. Badly damaged by a bomb in 1944, the dwellings and studio were demolished to make way for the LCC's Tor Gardens estate.

Sir William Llewellyn

Llewellyn (1858-1941) had to run away from home to become an artist and confounded his parents' direst predictions by becoming President of the Royal Academy and GCVO. Trained under Poynter (qv), he prospered as a portraitist and was elected RA for his depiction of Sir Aston Webb (qv). As PRA (1928-38) he promoted the cause of design in industry and showed a flair for organising international exhibitions and artistic cooperation which won him French, Dutch and Italian honours. Llewellyn lived at 3 Campden Hill in a purpose-built studio house of 1927. His ashes rest in St Paul's.

London Lighthouse, Lancaster Road

Established in 1986, this centre became Europe's largest residential and support facility for the treatment of victims of AIDs and HIV. Following a 75% fall in the death-rate from AIDS, the Lighthouse reformulated its strategy in 1999, abandoning residential care in favour of assisting victims to live with their condition and explore complementary therapies.

Sir David Low

Self-taught and inspired throughout his life by the work of Phil May (qv), Low (1891-1963), a New Zealander, was head-hunted in 1926 by Lord Beaverbrook for the *Evening Standard*.

As early as 1932 Churchill had already hailed Low as "the greatest of our political cartoonists" on account of both "the vividness of his political conceptions" and his "grand technique of draughtsmanship." Low's consistent ridiculing of Hitler and Mussolini got his paper banned in both Germany and Italy. By 1940 he was on the Gestapo's death list. Low's most famous creation was the reactionary xenophobe Colonel Blimp, whose name passed into the English language and who inspired one of the most brilliant films made by Michael Powell (qv). Low lived at 33 Melbury Court.

Charles Lucy (1814-73)

Lucy studied at the Ecole des Beaux-Arts under Delaroche, who was noted for his popular depictions of historical episodes. Lucy took the Puritans as his own favoured subject, selling many pictures on this theme to American purchasers and painting a mural of the Pilgrim Fathers for the Houses of Parliament. He was also commissioned to paint portraits of eminent men for presentation to the Victoria & Albert Museum. These included such past heroes as Cromwell and Nelson as well as contemporaries such as Cobden, Bright, Gladstone, Disraeli, Tennyson and Garibaldi. Lucy lived and died at 13 Ladbroke Crescent.

Thomas Babington Macaulay

Remembered, if at all, as an historian ("The history of England is emphatically the history of progress"), Lord Macaulay (1800-59) was in his own day revered as an essayist, a critic, a poet, an orator and a statesman. Sydney Smith described him as "like a book in breeches" and told Lady Holland that "he has occasional flashes of silence that make his conversation perfectly delightful." Born the eldest child of the Evangelical anti-slavery campaigner Zachary Macaulay, Macaulay had written his own Compendium of Universal History by the age of eight, plus a romance in three cantos in the style of Sir Walter Scott. Macaulay began reviewing books for the intellectual periodicals of the day at 23, was called to the bar at 26, elected MP at 30. He spent three years in India drafting a new legal code, virtually single-handed. In 1839 he became Secretary at War and in 1842 published his hugely successful *Lays of Ancient Rome*. The first two volumes of the *History of England from the Accession of James II* appeared in 1848 and were hailed as a masterpiece, with two further volumes appearing in 1855. Leaving Parliament in 1856, he retired, at the urging of his would-be neighbour the Duchess of Argyll, to Holly Lodge, Campden Hill, and discovered the delights of gardening in a location still judged to be "as rural as Roehampton". According to his biographer and nephew, Sir George Trevelyan, Macaulay had "refurnished his new abode in conformity with his sister's taste and his own notions of comfort." The dining room and drawing room were thought to be small but this mattered little to him because the library, where he passed most of his time, was large and gave directly onto a garden

91. *Thomas Babington Macaulay.*

strong audit ale. He prepared himself for his elevation to the peerage by memorising the primary and *secondary* titles of the entire membership of the House of Lords. On New Year's Day 1858 he recorded thankfully in his journal that "I am far from insensible to the pleasure of having fame, rank and this opulence which has come so late." Rural isolation restored his health and brought sleep "deeper and sweeter than it has been for years." The deepest sleep came peacefully and appropriately in his library as he was reading Thackeray's contribution to the first issue of the *Cornhill Magazine*.

In 1903 the London County Council, which had taken over the administration of the 'Blue Plaque' (then called the 'memorial tablet') scheme, decided to honour Macaulay with its first plaque. The then occupant of Holly Lodge, a Mrs Winkworth, who had made efforts to change it as little as possible, kept open house and former Prime Minister Lord Rosebery, no less, was invited to conduct the proceedings. In his speech Rosebery praised the LCC for improving the road to Kensington and praised the memorial tablet scheme for relieving the tedium of London streets which were "not ... too replete with interest", diverting the young "who need to have their imaginations turned in a more worthy direction than the Olympian (sic) Games" and not least for ensuring that those who came to pay quiet homage to the nation's great

whose "unbroken slope of verdure was worthy of the country house of a Lord Lieutenant." Macaulay referred to it as his "little paradise of shrubs and turf." Returning from abroad he once recorded smugly that "all the countries through which I have been travelling could not show such a carpet of soft rich green herbage as mine." Indeed, he became something of an obsessive in the matter of his lawn, waging unremitting war on dandelions. He ploughed on with his *History* (thanks to his painstaking thoroughness it only got as far as 1700) and wrote biographical entries for the *Encyclopaedia Britannica*. He entertained on a modest scale but thoughtfully, serving Dissenters with fillet of veal ("which he maintained to be the recognised Sunday dinner in good old Nonconformist families") and old Cambridge friends with did so at the correct address.

The seventh Earl of Airlie who had taken the house after Macaulay's death, had renamed it Airlie Lodge. The original name was subsequently reinstated until the house was demolished in 1968 to make way for extensions to Queen Elizabeth College.

Arthur Llewellyn Machen

Machen (1863-1947) left his native Wales at 17 and for eighteen months lived in a Clarendon Road garret so icy that he envied a nearby nightwatchman with a brazier. The other lodgers in the house were Armenian, Greek and Irish. Machen's solitary wanderings brought him repeatedly to Kensal Green cemetery (qv) "a terrible city of white gravestones and shattered pillars and granite urns and every sort of horrid heathenry." This "detested habitation of the dead" in fact proved to his taste as he became drawn to occultism, paganism and horror, genres which brought him literary success and recognition in the 1890s. Machen later became an actor and journalist and was inadvertently responsible for the Angel of Mons myth. After years of obscurity he now has a cult following.[44]

Colin MacInnes

Son of the novelist Angela Thirkell, MacInnes (1914-76) grew up in Australia. Returning to England, art school and army intelligence, he turned to the BBC, then journalism and produced two memorable novels. *City of Spades* (1957) was one of the first by a white writer to attempt to penetrate and depict the culture and experiences of Britain's recently-arrived Caribbean immigrants. *Absolute Beginners* (1959), in the mildly disdainful words of the *Oxford Companion to Literature* "described the new Bohemian underworld of Notting Hill, coffee bars, jazz clubs, drugs, drink and homosexuality." It concludes with a vivid description of the 1958 Notting Hill riots (qv). A 1985 film version – as a musical! – starring James Fox, David Bowie, Sade, Patsy Kensit, Mandy Rice-Davies and Ray Davies of The Kinks, was blamed for the demise of its hitherto celebrated production company, Goldcrest. Fox thought it "deserved to go down the toilet" – the film, not the company.

MacInnes' prose style was terse, direct, vernacular and very funny in an off-handedly bitter sort of way. He described 1950s Notting Hill as – "one of the few that's got left behind by the Welfare era and the Property-owning whatsit, both of them and is, in fact, nothing more than a stagnating slum. It's dying ... and that's the most important thing to remember about what goes on there."

Macinnes' papers are lodged at the University of Rochester.[45]

The Mangrove Nine

Repeated police raids on the Mangrove Restaurant in All Saints Road, alleged to be a focus for drug-dealing, led to an affray on 9th August 1970, following which nine men were arraigned at the Old Bailey. All were acquitted and the police were accused of fabricating evidence to secure convictions. In 1971, the Metro Four were likewise acquitted from charges of affray and assault following a police raid on the Metro Club in Notting Hill. These affairs contributed to the deterioration in relationships between the police and the black community in North Kensington, which came to a climax in the violence attending the carnival (qv) of 1976. Repeated subsequent raids on the Mangrove led to owner Frank Critchlow being arrested on (what proved to be trumped-up) drugs charges in 1987. Critchlow eventually extracted damages from the Home Office. The Mas Café now occupies the site of the Mangrove, whose name is perpetuated in that of the community information centre opposite.

Darcus Howe, a nephew of the Caribbean writer C L R James, was another of the Mangrove Nine and subsequently became a national figure as a broadcaster, journalist and activist. Paul Condon, Notting Hill police commander at the time of the Mangrove incident went on to receive a knighthood and become head of the Metropolitan Police.

Cardinal Manning

After seventeen years as an Anglican priest Henry Edward Manning (1808-92) converted to Catholicism in 1851 and in 1857 founded the Congregation of the Oblates of St Charles as a community of secular priests, with him-

92. *Cardinal Manning, from a portrait by G F Watts.*

self as its first superior. Based in Bayswater, they aimed to minister to the spiritual and educational needs of the poor of north-west London, many of them recent immigrants who had fled the Irish famine. The Oblates' work at Kensal Green was begun in two cottages which were used as a school. In 1857 Manning also established the convent of the Poor Clares Colettines at the corner of Westbourne Park Road and Ladbroke Grove. The buildings (1860-demolished 1970) were modelled on those of the Poor Clares at Bruges, from whom the first nuns were drawn. In 1857 Manning also founded a convent on the west side of Portobello Road, to be occupied from 1862 by nuns of the Third Order of St Francis. In 1870 a girls' orphanage was added to the complex. (The convent was then taken over in 1897 by Dominicans. In the 1970s it was bought by the Spanish government to become the Colegio Español, England's first Spanish school. The architect of both

convents was Henry Clutton (1819-93). In 1863 Manning founded St Charles College to educate upper class boys in the manner of "our English public schools". Initially established in Paddington, it relocated to St Charles Square in 1874. (In 1905 the buildings became a teacher-training college for women until it was evacuated in 1939) Manning succeeded Cardinal Wiseman as Archbishop of Westminster in 1865. He continued to place special emphasis on the needs of children, promoting the establishment of schools and orphanages and deferring the building of a cathedral for the metropolis. In 1877 Manning laid the foundation stone of the Carmelite Monastery of the Most Holy Trinity in St Charles Square and in 1881 of the church of Our Lady of Holy Souls, Bosworth Road. Manning also campaigned for total abstention but supported trade union rights. Disraeli made him the model for Cardinal Grandison in *Lothair*. Immense crowds attended Manning's burial at St Mary's, Kensal Green.[46]

John Charles Mason

A high official of the East India Company, Mason (1798-1881) undertook much secret diplomacy on its behalf and became its naval expert as well, organising the emergency transportation of troops during the great rebellion of 1857. Mason died at 12 Pembridge Gardens. His papers are deposited at the John Rylands University Library of Manchester.[47]

Phil May

A snappy dresser and a natural horseman, master-cartoonist Phil May (1864-1903) died, not yet forty, the victim of his weak constitution, unlimited bonhomie and unstinted alcohol. His artistic career began at twelve, painting scenery in a Leeds theatre and included a three year stint in Australia, during which he contributed 900 drawings to the Sydney *Bulletin*. These subsequently made him a hero to David Low (*qv*). May never had a drawing lesson in his life but acknowledged Linley Sambourne (*qv*) as his mentor. May, however, achieved an economy of line which gained the admiration of Whistler himself and inspired his admirers and acolytes to form the London Sketch Club. His stock-in-trade for *Punch* consisted of humorous sketches of Cockney characters. May lived for a while at 20 Holland Park Road, then known as Rowsley House and in 1899 at 11 Campden Hill Square. J J Shannon (*qv*) painted a full length portrait of May in hunting costume (May's childhood ambition had been to become a jockey) which was exhibited at the Royal Academy in 1901. When May died of cirrhosis of the liver a fellow employee of *Punch* declared "he was too good a fellow to go anywhere but heaven, although it will be a disappointment to the other place. The first thing he would have done is stand drinks all round." As a result of his generosity May, ever a soft touch for spongers, left his widow reliant on a Civil

93. *Phil May at work in his studio.*

List pension of £100 a year, despite a working lifetime of prolific output and substantial earnings. *Punch*, however, returned all his original drawings and £3,000 was realised from their sale.

Roger Mayne

Mayne's black and white photographic series of Southam Street, taken between 1956-61, depict a community in transition, the past represented by peeling paint on decaying homes and gangs of scruffy children playing in the street, the future by young West Indian men with broad-brimmed hats tilted at a jaunty angle. Southam Street as Mayne (1929-) knew it – 'romantic ... listless ... forbidding' – was demolished in 1969. Morrissey subsequently used Mayne's Southam Street series as a source for album covers and backdrops for stage-sets for his 1997 tour.[48]

James McBey (1883-1959)

Self-taught in etching, McBey gave up his safe job in a Scottish bank to travel. After serving as an official war artist with Allenby's Egyptian Expeditionary Force, McBey found himself in such demand that he commanded the highest prices ever paid to a living etcher – which enabled him to add a studio to the top of his home at 1 Holland Park Avenue. He later made his home in Morocco and became a US citizen.[49]

Stella McCartney

Stella McCartney (1971-) went straight from graduation at Central St Martin's to become chief designer at Chloe in Paris. Leaving in 2000 to develop her own label, in 2001-2 she bought and demolished Peake House, a former chapel and hostel for the homeless in Golborne Road, to redevelop the site as a house and studio.[50]

Richard Meinertzhagen

While serving with the King's African rifles in Kenya Meinertzhagen (1878-1967) discovered an entirely new species, the Great Forest Hog. Awarded the DSO for intelligence work in the Great War, he befriended T E Lawrence and attended the Paris Peace Conference. Resigning from the army in 1925 to combine ornithology with informal espionage, he returned to service in 1939 and at 62 was wounded rescuing men from Dunkirk. An enthusiastic Zionist, in 1948, at 70, he fought in a lethal skirmish at Haifa. In retirement at 17 Kensington Park Gardens Meinertzhagen polished his diaries for publication in four volumes of autobiography and compiled classic works of reference on the ornithology of Egypt and Arabia. The 76 volumes of Meinertzhagen's diaries were deposited at Rhodes House, Oxford; their reliability has become a matter of scholarly controversy. Meinertzhagen (played by Julian Firth) was appropriated, in a supporting role to T E Lawrence, as a character in *Young Indiana Jones and the Phantom Train of Doom*.

Melbury Road

The Valhalla of high-profile Victorian artists, this grand, sweeping avenue, laid out from 1875 onwards, contains the former homes of Val Prinsep, Sir Luke Fildes, Marcus Stone, Sir Hamo Thornycroft, William Burges, G F Watts, William Holman Hunt and film-makers Michael Powell and Michael Winner. Benjamin Britten *(qv)*

94. 14 Melbury Road, built for Colin Hunter, 1876-8. The architect was J J Stevenson.

lived in the flats at No. 22 (1948-53); during this fruitful period he wrote *The Little Sweep*, *Spring Symphony*, *Billy Budd* and *Gloriana* and founded the Aldeburgh Festival.

Archibald Menzies

A naval surgeon by profession and naturalist by vocation, Menzies (1754-1842) discovered three new species of plant and three of sea creatures. He died at Ladbroke Terrace and was buried at Kensal Green.[51]

Mercury Theatre

Built as the Congregational Sunday School attached to Kensington Temple (qv) and known as the Horbury Hall, the building was bought by Ashley Dukes (qv) out of his earnings from *A Man with a Load of Mischief* and converted into a theatre, known from 1933 as the Mercury. It was intended as a showcase for new and uncommercial plays and as a base for the ballet company run by Dukes' wife Marie Rambert (qv), thus becoming the first ever permanent home of ballet in England. The co-presence of the two was highly significant. The critic Arthur Haskell recognized this as early as 1938 when he praised Marie Rambert for showing "that a dancing school must be something more than a physical-training ground; it must be a cultural centre." Haskell also recognised that whereas large theatres with large overheads could not afford to take risks a miniature one had to do so in order to survive because it could

95. *The Mercury Theatre in Ladbroke Road, the first home of Ballet Rambert.*

not compete with conventionally commercial rivals. In 1935 the first London production of T S Eliot's *Murder in the Cathedral* was staged at the Mercury. It ran for 225 nights before transferring to the West End. Verse drama became a noted feature of the Mercury's distinctive genre under E Martin Browne and his Pilgrim Players. The offbeat tradition was continued with works by Eugene O'Neill and Christopher Fry, children's plays and plays in French. In 1948 the Mercury provided the setting for a performance of Act 2 of *Swan Lake* in Michael Powell's (qv) *The Red Shoes*, with Moira Shearer playing guest ballerina Victoria Page, and Marie Rambert appearing as herself. From 1953 to 1966 the theatre was only used by the ballet and thereafter occasionally by visiting companies. It was converted to a private home in the 1980s.

Montessori

In 1946 Margaret Homfray and Phoebe Child, formerly students and latterly colleagues of the Italian educationist Maria Montessori, established Britain's first permanent Montessori training college in St Mark's Road, North Kensington. A nursery school was opened in Chepstow Villas in 1948. The venture was established as a trust in 1954 when it moved to 15 Dawson Place. In 1969 it removed to larger premises at 22-24 Prince's Gate.[52]

Moray Lodge

Built by John Tasker in 1817, the house was originally called West Lodge. When John Malcolmson, a Scot, took up occupation in 1844, he changed the name to Moray Lodge. From 1861 to 1893 it was the home of Arthur Lewis, of Lewis and Allenby, silk mercers. Lewis, a Captain in the Artists' Rifles, founder of the Arts Club, and his actress wife Kate Terry, were the grandparents of Sir John Gielgud. They entertained lavishly, attracting such guests as Dickens, Trollope, Millais, Thackeray, Rossetti, Arthur Sullivan, George du Maurier and near neighbours Holman Hunt and Val Prinsep (*qqv*). Collectively they constituted The Moray Minstrels who met at the house for "billiards, singing and to go to Bohemia for a night." The soirees at Moray Lodge featured in du Maurier's hit novel *Trilby* (1894). In 1902 the house was used as a temporary lodging for the Maharajah of Jaipur who had come to attend the coronation of Edward VII, accompanied by a retinue of two hundred and a white cow.

Subsequently enlarged and modernised, Moray Lodge was vast. Standing at the summit of Campden Hill, approached by a long avenue, guarded by two lodges and surrounded by extensive grounds (with peach house and vinery), it had four panelled reception rooms, twenty bedrooms, half a dozen bathrooms, a service lift, garaging for six large cars (with seven rooms overhead for chauffeurs) and two tennis courts. Moray Lodge was requisitioned by the authorities during World War Two and retained until demolished in 1955 to make way for the construction of Holland Park School (*qv*).

Charles Langridge Morgan

Morgan (1894-1958) lived at 16 Campden Hill Square (*qv*) from 1931 until his death. A former President of the Oxford University Dramatic Society, he was drama critic of *The Times* (1926-39) and a prize-winning novelist whose work gained greater regard in France than in the UK.

Sir Oswald Mosley (1896-1980)

Following the 1958 Notting Hill 'riots' (*qv*) Britain's veteran fascist leader returned from self-imposed exile to stand as Union Movement candidate for North Kensington in the 1959 election. Castigating Caribbean immigrants for worsening the housing situation, undercutting wages and sexual predation, Mosley (1896-1980) advocated a policy of repatriation. The voters of North Kensington, recently outraged by the murder of Kelso Cochrane (*qv*) were unpersuaded and Mosley came bottom of the poll, with 2,821 votes out of 34,912 and lost his deposit. This had never happened to him before and he attempted to bring a court action to query the result, alleging electoral irrregularities. Nothing came of this. Mosley's Union Movement continued to maintain a presence in the area and in 1962 Mosley, on his way to address a meeting in Ridley Road, was knocked down and kicked by a gang of men. Mosley's perverse political odyssey ended with a final electoral debacle at Shoreditch in 1966.[53]

Andrew Murray (1812-78)

Abandoning the law and Scotland for science and London, Murray (1812-78) became scientific director of the Royal Horticultural Society. His main areas of exper-

96. Sir Oswald Mosley leading a group of supporters of the British Union of Fascists, 1938.

tise were entomology and conifers. A trip to the American West severely impaired his health and he died at 67 Bedford Gardens with much scholarly work uncompleted.

Sir Isaac Newton

The great scientist lived the last two years of his long life (1642-1727) in a house on the site now covered by Bullingham Mansions on the west side of Kensington Church Street.

Erskine Nicol

A notably dour Scot, who paradoxically specialised in painting humorous scenes of Irish and Scotttish peasant life, Nicol (1825-1904) lived at 24 Dawson Place, Pembridge Square from 1864 until ill-health ended his career in 1885.

Niddry Lodge

A stuccoed, detached house which once stood on the site of the present Town Hall,

Niddry Lodge was first occupied in 1831 by General Sir John Fraser (1760-1843), until his death. Fraser lost his right leg at the age of twenty-two but still commanded with distinction an African regiment composed of military offenders. He married for the second time at the age of eighty. The next occupant was the Dowager Countess of Hopetoun who named the house after one of her late consort's lesser titles, Baron Niddry. Following her death in 1854 the property was occupied by John Francis Campbell (1821-85), clan chief of the Campbells of Islay. Campbell devoted much of his life to collecting Highland folk-stories and also invented a device for recording the intensity of sunshine. Niddry Lodge was demolished in 1972.

Norland Estate

The 52 acres developed as the Norland estate originally constituted the grounds of

Norlands, a house which stood approximately on the site of 130 Holland Park Avenue and was destroyed by fire in 1825. In 1740 Norlands had been inherited by the infant Edward Burnaby Greene (died 1788), together with an annual income of £4,000 and a Westminster brewery. Greene's inheritance gave him the leisure to make turgid translations from the classics and compose feeble verse which brought him more ridicule than reputation. Meanwhile his wealth became an enormous debt which forced him into humble lodgings and was undischarged at his death. From 1792 until 1839 the Norlands estate was occupied by the Vulliamy family *(qv)* and then developed by solicitor Charles Richardson with Robert Cantwell (1792-1858) as surveyor, until Joseph Dunning took over in 1841. Cantwell's own designs for houses included the imposing Royal Crescent (1842-3), Addison Avenue and Norland Square. After improving the drainage of the locality work began in 1839. Five hundred houses were erected in the 1840s. The 1851 census revealed that they appealed most strongly to female annuitants, implying that they were rather too far from town to suit men of business. The failure to let or sell sufficient of the houses which had been so rapidly erected ruined Richardson who removed to Glasgow and became a patent medicine salesman. Writer and currency reformer Jonathan Duncan the younger (1799-

97. Norland Square, c.1905.

1865) lived at 33 Norland Square and the Irish popular historian and novelist Joseph Fitzgerald Molloy (1858-1908) at No. 20.

Norland House Military Academy

This academy was opened in 1761 by Thomas Marquois, a self-styled 'Professor of Artillery and Fortification' on a twelve acre site now bounded by Portland Road, Norland Square and Penzance Place. Marquois was succeeded in 1765 by Abraham Elim who shifted the emphasis towards a civil as much as military education for 'sons of the gentry'. In 1785 the new proprietor, Lt. Bartholomew Reynolds reverted to a military emphasis, acquired the patronage of the Prince of Wales and accordingly restyled the establishment as a 'Royal Military Academy'. It was recommended that students enter before the age of ten to be ready to graduate at sixteen. (Students were, however, taken at any age under fifteen.) For such a course the annual fee was sixty guineas, plus an entrance premium of a further ten. Alternatively one could opt for the civilian core curriculum (Latin, Greek, French, Writing and Arithmetic) for thirty guineas plus five guineas entrance, to include board. To this could be added, for a guinea premium and half a guinea a month, electives chosen from Fortification, Mathematics, Navigation, Drawing, Geography, Dancing and Fencing. Riding cost two guineas premium and two guineas a month. The facilities were as extensive as the course of instruction was varied. There was a covered riding-house, an outdoor riding arena and separate playing areas for cricket, skittles and fives, all set in walled grounds. The establishment also practised a considerable degree of self-sufficiency, having its own kitchen garden, two canals stocked with fish, four cows, a hen house and a brew house. In 1787 the students proved their worth when fire broke out nearby, destroying three houses. A Norland contingent was swiftly mustered to guard against looting and recovered a hoard of stolen plate. In 1788 the freeholder Edward Burnaby Greene died in debt. Norland House closed in 1792 and its contents were sold off. As this was the year that war broke out with revolutionary France there were at least exciting, if lethal, opportunities opening up for staff and students alike. Benjamin Vulliamy (qv) bought the whole of the Norland estate and took up residence in the house which had provided the residential accommodation for the Academy. It was destroyed by fire in 1825.

One of the most illustrious graduates of Norland House was Major-General Sir Robert Rollo Gillespie (1766-1814). A diminutive man, he once killed six robbers single-handed, put down the sepoy mutiny at Vellore in 1806, conquered Djakarta with a force one twentieth the size of its garrison and was killed storming the fort of Kalunga in India.

Norland Nannies

In their distinctive brown uniforms Norland Nannies are the creme-de-la-creme of their calling. A swift trawl through the Internet reveals that Cunard boasts about employing them and an anarchist website equates employing one with the epitome of elitism. The Norland Institute was founded in 1892 by Emily Ward (née Lord) (1850-1930) to train child-carers to a professional standard. Her career began as the infant class teacher at Notting Hill High School (qv). In 1876, with the consent of her headmistress (who once expressed the wish that children could be born aged ten), she founded Norland Place School at 9 Norland Place (now 166 Holland Park Avenue) as a feeder establishment to take children up to ten. It was run on the lines developed by the German educational theorist Friedrich Froebel and received a first class commendation from the Froebel Society of Great Britain in 1879. Emily later became President of that Society and was a founder member of the Kindergarten Association. By 1887, when the school opened a senior section, it had already begun training teachers. In 1890 Emily Ward married a retired Shanghai tea merchant, Walter Ward, who helped finance her future efforts. They moved to Ladbroke Grove, leaving her vacated rooms at Norland Place School to become the first home of the Norland Institute. This initiative was launched with skilful networking and press coverage

98. The rural scene of Notting Hill c.1750.

to attract potential students and employers. Mrs Ward had a tremendous flair for public relations and would attract the support of Madame de Montessori, Mrs. Winston Churchill and Ramsay MacDonald. It proved unnecessary to advertise but was soon necessary to move into larger premises at 19 Holland Park Terrace (now 29 Holland Park Avenue). In 1900 the Institute moved to 10 Pembridge Square, later acquiring No. 11. Every three months up to 25 recruits, aged from 15 to 30 and drawn from the professional rather than the artisan classes, were admitted after being carefully screened and taking a General Knowl-edge examination. The training programme initially consisted of six weeks of residential training (cookery, laundry, light household chores, lectures, needlework, kindergarten games, singing, stories), six more of kinder-garten experience, three months on a hospital chil-dren's ward then three months probation with an employer who assessed the trainee's neatness, cleanli-ness, punctuality, tact and temper. Successful comple-tion of the course led to a certificate and from 1902 a badge, with, from 1911, bars for long service. Mrs Ward set the highest standards and expected the badges to be treated as heirlooms; selling off the distinctive uniforms (made by needy gentlewomen) was a disciplinary offence. By 1914 the Institute had pro-duced 1,400 'Norlanders'. Norland nannies really were dedicated to their calling; a survey in 1935 found that only 25% had married. Norland, after several moves, is now located near Bath. In 1892 the course cost £36, in 2002 £24,000 – roughly equal to a year's prospective earnings.

Notting Dale in the Nineties

Charles Booth's massive sur-vey of work, wealth and poverty in the capital – *Life and Labour of the People of London (1886-1903)* – characterised Notting Dale as a "bag, bone and bottle district" to which scavengers returned with their pickings from Kensington and St John's Wood. Organ grinders also hired instruments there but most inhabitants were dismissed as cadgers and loafers although there were also "a few skilled mechanics among them simply too lazy to work." Sirdar Road and Kenilworth Street were full of lodging houses, many housing former residents of Lisson Grove, whose homes had been demolished to make way for the Great Central Railway.

Notting Hill Housing Trust

Established in 1963 by the Reverend Bruce Frederick, founder of Shelter, the trust re-housed 3,500 people in the first decade of its existence.

Notting Hill – The Movie

Boy (Will = travel bookshop owner = Hugh Grant) meets/ loses/gets girl (Anna = film mega-star = Julia Roberts), supported by fine ensemble cast, notably newcomer Rhys Ifans as crackpot Welsh scruff, Spike. The real Travel Bookshop is in Blenheim Crescent. No. 142 Nicholls Antique Arcade (now Gong, a furnishings shop) next to the butcher's, stood in for it in the film. The exterior of Grant's flat was represented by 280 Westbourne Park Road. The restaurant scene was shot in the cards and poster shop Portfolio, at 93 Golborne Road. The wedding reception was shot in the Hempel Hotel's Zen garden in Craven Hill Gardens. The director of this film made in 1999, was Roger Michell, producer Duncan Kenworthy and writer Richard Curtis, a local resident. (The house with the blue door – 280 Westbourne Park Road – where Will lives, was the Curtis residence, formerly a chapel, with a courtyard garden, a galleried mezzanine and a reception room covering a thousand square feet. The door was later auctioned at Christie's after he sold the house (asking price £1.3m), whose new door became black. Curtis, also writer of *Four Weddings and a Funeral*, includes among other credits *Mr. Bean*, *Blackadder, French & Saunders* and the screenplay for *Bridget Jones's Diary*. As the moving spirit behind Comic Relief's Red Nose Day annual fundraiser Curtis was awarded the CBE in 2000.

Notting Hill (and Ealing) High School

Founded by the Girls Public Day School Trust in 1873, the school took over buildings in Norland Square built for a boys' establishment in 1867.

99. The High School for Girls, Norland Square, c.1904.

100. The Notting Hill turnpike gate. From a watercolour by Paul Sandby, 1793.

The first headmistress Miss Harriet Morant Jones began with one assistant and ten children. When she retired in 1900, there were twenty teachers and 400 girls. William Morris thought well enough of the school to send his daughters there. Violet Hunt *(qv)* was also a pupil, as were the nutritionist and centenarian Dame Harriet Chick (1875-1977), Viscountess Rhondda (1883-1958), founder and editor of the political review *Time and Tide*, and the distinguished historian Elizabeth Wiskemann (1899-1971). The Norland Institute *(qv)* for training nannies was founded by a former infants' teacher at the school. The school moved to larger premises in Ealing in 1930-1.[54]

Observatory Gardens

This street's name commemorates what was, at the time of its construction in 1826, the world's finest private observatory. Its builder, Sir James South FRS (1785-1867) was an astronomer of great talent much given to quarrelling. Trained for surgery, he married advantageously enough at 31 to devote his time to star-gazing, receiving the gold medal of the Astronomical Society and the Copley medal of the Royal Society in the year in which he shifted his operations from the smoky surroundings of Southwark to the bracing heights of Campden Hill, moving into an eighteenth century mansion which had been the family home of the Phillimores. A founder of the Astronomical Society, South was elected President in 1829 but when its royal charter was drafted in 1831 in his name a virulent dispute arose among leading members and South withdrew from the Society and cut himself off from most of his colleagues. Soothed somewhat by a knighthood and a civil list pension of £300 in recognition of his researches, in 1831 South imported from France the world's largest telescope but when it proved inoperative in situ refused to pay the expert commissioned to install its mounting. Protracted proceedings ended with judgment entirely against South at a cost of £8,000. In fury he broke up the instrument in dispute and auctioned off its components in his garden. He subsequently commissioned the celebrated

101. A plaque describing the origins of the street name.

ROYAL BOROUGH OF KENSINGTON AND CHELSEA
OBSERVATORY GARDENS
DERIVES ITS NAME FROM THE OBSERVATORY THAT SIR JAMES SOUTH THE ASTRONOMER BUILT HERE IN 1831 AND WHICH CONTAINED FOR A TIME THE LARGEST TELESCOPE IN THE WORLD. AFTER THE ASTRONOMERS DEATH THE SITE WAS SOLD TO THOMAS CAWLEY WHO BUILT THE EXISTING HOUSES IN THE 1880'S.

engineer Isambard Kingdom Brunel to enlarge his observatory and quarrelled with him over the bill for that. South did little important work thereafter, contenting himself with acrimonious letters to the press and a defamatory pamphlet against his old opponents in the Astronomical Society. Cambridge gave him an honorary degree in 1863. He became partially blind and deaf and finally succumbed to a painful disease, still living at his observatory on Campden Hill. Observatory Gardens was built shortly after his demise, driving straight through South's former domain.

Feargus O'Connor

O'Connor (1794-1855) was a charismatic (if seldom coherent) orator, who claimed descent from the ancient kings of Ireland. He died impoverished and demented in his sister's lodging-house at 18 Notting Hill. In 1837 he had founded the *Northern Star* as a weekly radical paper to denounce the new Poor Law and the factory system. In 1838 he was instrumental in uniting diverse groups to create the Chartist movement, demanding a far-reaching democratisation of the constitution. O'Connor's egotism led him to quarrel with practically every other Chartist leader but his rabble-rousing skills sustained his popularity with the rank and file. O'Connor's agitational career ended in fiasco as his 'back to the land' smallholding project foundered and the great Chartist assembly at Kennington in 1848 dispersed

102. *Feargus O'Connor.*

aimlessly. Increasingly a victim of dementia and drink, he was committed to an asylum after grossly insulting an MP in the House of Commons. Against the wishes of his doctors O'Connor was taken in by his sister in 1854 and stayed under her care until his death. A public collection was needed to pay for the funeral at Kensal Green cemetery. Mourners gathered at the Prince Albert public house and marched in column to the burial which some contemporaries allege to have attracted a crowd of fifty thousand.

George Orwell

Orwell (1903-50) lived at No. 22 Portobello Road in 1927-8, after resigning from the Burma police. Determined to become a writer he decided he needed to be in London,

103. *George Orwell.*

although he was later to despise, and hold himself aloof from, London literary circles. Orwell's landlady was such a crashing snob that when the occupants of the house found themselves locked out she refused to borrow her next door neighbour's ladder to get in through a still open upper window on the grounds that she had no intention of breaking her fourteen year track record of completely ignoring them. Orwell was duly despatched to fetch a ladder from a relative over a mile away.

While living here Orwell began to dress as a tramp (changing in the pottery studio next door) to disguise himself for the East End explorations which eventually found their literary incarnation in *Down and Out in Paris and London* (1933). In 1936 Victor Gollancz (*qv*) despatched Orwell to the North of England for the research which underpinned *The Road to Wigan Pier* (1937), published for his recently-founded Left Book Club. The £500 advance was equal to two year's normal earnings for Orwell and enabled him to get married.[55]

Thomas Page

Initially working as a draughtsman for the architect Edward Blore, Page (1803-77) then assisted the Brunels in the building of their Thames tunnel. As a civil engineer Page was responsible for building Chelsea Bridge and the new (present) Westminster Bridge, the latter skilfully phased to avoid any interruption of traffic. In 1852-3 Page had a fantastical house built in Aubrey Road, Tower Cressy, in what one might call semi-medieval rather than pseudo-medieval style. Named in homage to the Black Prince, it sported that hero's heraldic emblems.

The building later became a home for children awaiting adoption and then The Princess Alice Nursery Training School. Tower Cressy was severely damaged by a bomb in 1944 and demolished thereafter.

Pembridge Square

The area around Pembridge Square (1856-64) was developed between 1840 and 1870, mainly by Bayswater builders Francis and William Radford. Designated as a Conservation Area in 1969, it has since 1972 been safeguarded by the Pembridge Association. Pembridge Square was home to Field Marshal Sir John Fox Burgoyne, scientist J H Gladstone and to the Norland Nannies *(qqv)*.[56]

104. *Tower Cressy in Aubrey Road, the home of engineer Thomas Page and then of designer Christopher Dresser (1834-1904) from c.1869 until 1882.*

Performance

Starring James Fox as a vicious gangster on the run and Mick Jagger as drug-taking dropout rock musician Turner Purple, this film was shot (1968, released 1971) largely in Powis Square. Hailed as powerful and absorbing, it was held to have captured the frenetic atmosphere of the day perhaps too well. Two of the film's stars became heroin addicts, the writer killed himself and Fox took to religion and made no films for the next decade. Interviewed a quarter of a century later Fox admitted that, despite extensive analysis by film theorists and critics, no one, including debut-director Nicholas Roeg, could explain what *Performance* was actually about.

Glyn Philpot

Glyn Warren Philpot (1884-1937), like his fellow residents at Lansdowne House *(qv)*, Shannon and Ricketts *(qqv)*, was a product of the Lambeth Art School. His passions included Spain and sketching black male models (notably his manservant Henry Thomas) but he was in constant demand as a portraitist both in Britain and the USA. He had his first one-man show when he was just nineteen. His portrait subjects included Siegfried Sassoon, Oswald Mosley *(qqv)*, and Prime Minister Stanley Baldwin. Commissioned to paint the king of Egypt (for £3,000 plus expenses), Philpot was enthralled by North Africa. In the 1930s he turned to sculpture and water-colours. When Philpot died suddenly of heart failure, his disciple Vivian Forbes (1891-1937), another denizen of Lansdowne House (1923-35), committed suicide after Philpot's funeral. The National Portrait Gallery held a major retrospective of Philpot's work in 1985.[57]

John Hungerford Pollen

By the time Pollen (1820-1902) worked alongside William Morris and Rossetti on the abortive scheme to decorate the Oxford Union with fresco in 1858, he was already an ex-don and and ex-priest. From that year he lived at 11 Pembridge Crescent. Apart from providing frescoes for Alton Towers, Pollen undertook many decorative commissions for churches and was appointed to the staff of the Victoria & Albert Museum, where he lectured on historical ornament and catalogued books on art. He was also a keen member of the artists' corps of volunteers headed by Lord Leighton *(qv)*.

James Pope-Hennessy

(Richard) James (Arthur) Pope-Hennessey (1916-74) lived in a maisonette at 9 Ladbroke Grove from 1942 until his murder in 1974. The son of a general and a forceful Catholic mother, Pope-Hennessy left Balliol without a degree but won the Hawthornden Prize for his first book, *London Fabric* (1939) and served in military intelligence during the Second World War. He then wrote travel books and biographies, his life of Queen Mary earning him a CVO. *Verandah* (1964) sketches the turbulent life of his grandfather, the controversial colonial governor Sir John Pope-Hennessy, who was Trollope's model for Phineas Finn. Pope-Hennessy later returned the compliment with a biography of Trollope. The author's sparkling conversation had long made him a welcome guest for many hostesses but his personal preference was for casual homosexual liaisons, regardless of the risk he repeatedly ran of blackmail, violence and disgrace. Increasing alcoholism was accompanied by an indiscriminate choice of partners and together these caused his destruction. Imprudent reference to a handsome advance received for a projected biography of Sir Noel Coward tempted assailants to murder him at his home, choking him with his own hairnet.

Portobello Road

Portobello, scene of a famous victory in the opening phase of the Anglo-Spanish conflict

105. George Orwell's house at 22 Portobello Road.

known as the *War of Jenkins' Ear*, gave its name to a farm, road and market in Notting Hill, a suburb of Edinburgh and innumerable pubs throughout the land. On 21 November 1739 Vice-Admiral Edward Vernon (1684-1757), commanding a force of just six ships, stormed and took the fortress of Puerto Bello in Panama. The exploit made him a national hero and his surname became a given name as patriots named their sons in his honour.

Portobello Road, originally Portobello Lane, was once a winding country pathway leading from the turnpike gate at Notting Hill to Portobello farmhouse. When the Ladbroke estate began building in the 1840s long ranges of terraced houses were built along the east side of Kensington Park Road to "shut off Portobello Lane from contact with the well-to-do inhabitants further west."

Portobello Road itself was

106. Marks and Spencer at 233 Portobello Road in 1905.

107. Portobello Farmhouse c.1864. From a drawing by W Wellings.

built up quite quickly between *c.*1854 and 1872.

A street market was established by the 1870s. (By 1900 there were others in Kenley Street, Sirdar Road, Norland Road, Crescent Street and Golborne Road.) Like most London markets Portobello's main purpose was the supply of provisions but it did also feature gypsies dealing in horses and herbs. The presence of the market may have been handy for householders but it also precipitated a rapid social decline, with houses in Colville Gardens being already sub-divided for multiple occcupation by 1881. By 1893 the sprawling expansion of the stall-holders was causing conflict with neighbouring shopkeepers but no official licences were granted to stall-holders to regulate their activities until 1927. Local resident Monica Dickens described the character of the market in that decade in her memoirs. The temporary closure of Caledonian Market in 1948 led to a mass-migration of antique dealers from there to Portobello Road, imparting a very different character to Saturdays. The Portobello Antique Dealers association was founded in 1985 and now numbers over 1,500 members who collectively constitute what is claimed to be the world's largest antiques market. The road's famous residents include George Orwell (*qv*) at No. 22 and poet Roger McGough. The Manna Cafe was until 1991 the premises of fine art printers Petersberg Press whose clients included Henry Moore and David

Hockney. Richard Branson first set up Virgin Records *(qv)*, in what is now an emporium, next door.[58]

The Potteries

The Potteries, lying between the Norland estate and Notting Barns Farm, an area now bounded at its extremes by Walmer Road to the north and St James's Gardens to the south, had acquired its name by 1833. By the time of the second cholera outbreak of 1848-9 its insanitary condition had become so notorious that Dickens *(qv)* ran a special feature on it in the first issue of his magazine *Household Words*. The manufacture of pottery, mostly drain-pipes, tiles and flower pots, followed on from the making of bricks to supply the local building boom and was in existence by 1824 and continued until 1863. Samuel Lake, displaced from Tottenham Court Road, had already established his pig-keeping business in the area by then and was joined by other pig-keepers ousted from Paddington by building activity. The pig-keepers were largely sustained by recycling refuse collected from their bourgeois neighbours up the hill – "the best of it we eats ourselves or gives it to a neighbour. The fat is boiled down and the rest we gives to the pigs." In 1838 Poor Law Commissioners declared that some of the cottages in the area were actually built over stagnant ponds. In 1849 it was reported that the 1,056 residents lived 130 to the acre, sharing their space with 3,000 pigs and achieving a life

108. *A tile kiln in the Potteries area, 1824.*

109. *Cottages in the Potteries, 1855.*

expectancy of eleven years seven months compared with a metropolitan average of thirty-seven. During the first ten months of that year twenty-one people died of cholera or diarrhoea. Criss-crossed with foul ditches and unpaved streets, pockmarked with pits dug for brick-earth and filled with stinking stagnation, the area was targeted for remedial action by Kensington's first medical officer, Dr Francis Godrich who characterised it as "one of the most deplorable spots not only in Kensington but in the whole of the Metropolis. The amount of sickness and death may be equalled but scarcely exceeded by any part of England." Godrich found many of the inhabitants living in

110. *The Prince of Wales in Pottery Lane, 2004.*

converted railway carriages and discovered that the smallpox death-rate was ten times higher than in surrounding districts.

The 1860s at last witnessed the opening of schools, the paving of streets, the construction of proper sewers – and the arrival of a colony of gypsies *(qv)*. Population density rose to 180 per acre, however, and the area remained lethal for the under-fives. By 1878 Godrich's successor, Dr Dudfield, had evicted the pigs to become Hammersmith's problem. The previous notoriety of the area and the intrusion of the Hammersmith & City Line *(qv)* condemned it to be developed with dense rows of artisan cottages. Against such a background local residents made a living as best they could. Some worked the streets 'up West' as costers or flower-sellers or prostitutes. Others worked less favoured thoroughfares as coalmen, rag and bone men or bookies' runners. Local stables em-

ployed men and boys as drivers, to care for horses and to wash or mend vehicles. Noisome trades included rendering offal into fat and oil or smoking fish. Women homebound by the need to care for infants or invalids earned a pittance washing and ironing clothes or painting toys, a tradition of 'homework' which continued into the middle of the twentieth century.

Not until 1888 were public baths and wash-houses provided at the junction of Silchester and Lancaster Roads. Avondale Park was belatedly opened in 1892. In 1893, however, the *Daily News* could still denigrate the locality as 'A West-End Avernus', provoking Dudfield to discover that there were 723 people crammed into just 11 lodging-houses and that death-rates were no better than they had been in the 1850s. Infant mortality stood at a staggering 432 per 1,000 live births, compared with the London average of 161. Dudfield's pleas for more staff were, however, rejected by the Vestry, which actually cut the number of inspectors from seven to six – each responsible for the sanitary welfare of 28,000 people. When the Kensington Vestry was superseded by Kensington Borough Council it rapidly appointed four extra inspectors and bought up dwellings for improvement. In 1896-8 the death rate in what had been euphemistically designated the 'Notting Dale Special Area' stood at 50.4 per 1,000. By 1907 it had been cut to 30.2

111. *10 Kensington Church Walk, where Ezra Pound stayed at the end of 1909.*

Ezra Pound

Pound (1885-1972) moved into a first floor room at No. 10 Kensington Church Walk, off Holland Street, at the end of 1909. The rent was eight shillings (40p) a week plus the willingness to make deliveries occasionally for his grocer landlord. That winter J M Dent accepted Pound's *Spirit of Romance* and he gave a course of lectures at Regent Street Polytechnic (now the University of Westminster). Pound described his circumstances in a poem of 1916 *The Bathtub*. Ford Madox Ford *(qv)* personally showed the American newcomer round the area, a kindness recalled almost forty years later in *Canto LXXX* (1948). Pound must have cut rather a bizarre figure in that respectable locality, dressed in a flowing cloak, sporting an ear-ring and ringing the sartorial changes with items of his own devising such as hand-painted ties or trousers made from green billiard-table baize.

One of Pound's first guests was William Carlos Williams. D H Lawrence also stayed there. Robert Frost called in and introduced himself.

Pound found rooms opposite for the American poet Hilda Doolittle who had been a fellow student at the University of Pennsylvania, and for the English poet Richard Aldington. In his 1929 novel *Death of a Hero* Aldington based Mr Upjohn and his studio on Pound and his room. Together the three of them constituted themselves as a new poetic movement, Les Imagistes. In 1914 Pound published his first article on art, devoted to the sculpture of Henri Gaudier-Brzeska and Jacob Epstein. In March of that same year he moved to a small flat, 5 Holland Place Chambers and a month later married Dorothy Shakespear in St Mary Abbots (qv). In September they were visited for tea by a newcomer to England, T S Eliot, who read them *The Love Song of Alfred J. Prufrock*. Pound did what he could to advance Eliot's literary career and, after an introduction through Yeats, did the same for James Joyce. Pound's combative side led him to challenge the poet Lascelles Abercrombie to a duel. Knowing Pound to be a skilled fencer Abercrombie suggested they should fling their unsold volumes of verse at each other. In 1920 Pound left London for Paris, having composed the first three of the *Cantos* which were to be regarded as his greatest work. He came back to London only once, in 1965, for T S Eliot's memorial service.

Michael Powell

Described by Martin Scorsese as the "greatest intellectual influence" on his own work,

film director Michael Powell (1905-90) has been increasingly recognised as the unsung genius of British cinema. Educated at Dulwich College, he soon quit banking for filming, working with Hitchcock and Michael Balcon. Alexander Korda teamed him with the exiled Austrian Emeric Pressburger as scriptwriter. Together they made seventeen films, including the war's first propaganda coup, *49th Parallel, The Life and Death of Colonel Blimp*, the imaginatively supernatural *A Matter of Life and Death* and *The Red Shoes*. Powell's later works ranged from mainstream blockbusters like *The Battle of the River Plate* to cinematic versions of opera and ballet and involved him in collaborations in the USA, USSR and Australia. Powell, who had explored the wilder reaches of Albania and Burma and at 79 married Scorsese's editor, Thelma Schoonmaker, forty years his junior, listed his main recreation as "leaning on gates". He lived in Melbury Road in the house formerly occupied by the artist Marcus Stone (qv) and used it as a location for some of the scenes in the film *Peeping Tom* (1960) which had a major influence on Scorsese. No. 5 Melbury Road also featured in the film. Powell wrote two volumes of autobiography *A Life in the Movies* (1986) and *A Million Dollar Movie* (1992).[59]

Sir Edward Poynter

After resigning as Director of the National Gallery and having been elected President of the Royal Academy,

Poynter (1836-1919) lived at No. 70 Addison Road from 1905 until his death. Poynter's versatility had enabled him to produce not only monumental oils and accomplished water-colours but also sculpture, mosaics, frescoes and tile-work and to undertake decorative projects at Waltham Abbey, the Houses of Parliament and the V & A. As first head of the Slade and Principal of the National Art Training School at South Kensington, Poynter also exerted a lasting influence by promoting the French approach to art teaching through his appointments of Alphonse Legros and Jacques Dalou. When Graham Robertson (qv) was told that the reserved and cantankerous Poynter had his heart in the right place, he doubted whether his liver was. Created a baronet, Poynter was buried in St Paul's.

Val Prinsep

The first 'artist's house', built as such, to go up in London and thus to initiate what was to become the artists' colony of Melbury Road was No.1 Holland Park Road (from 1908 No. 14), built in 1865 for Valentine Cameron Prinsep (1838-1904) to the designs of Philip Webb for £2,000. Webb had recently designed the revolutionary pseudo-medieval Red House in Bexley for William Morris, an inspiration substantially reflected in his designs for Prinsep. The studio – 40' x 25' – took up most of the first floor. Pevsner hails No. 14 as a "remarkably early example of the revival of red brick for

London houses" but regrets the obscuring of the original profile by Webb's further additions of 1877 and 1892. Prinsep's artistic career was virtually determined for him by growing up in the Little Holland House menage alongside G F Watts (qv). Prinsep studied in Paris alongside Whistler, Poynter (qv) and George du Maurier, who, half a lifetime later, would make him the model for Taffy in his novel *Trilby*. Burne-Jones, Rossetti and Browning were early acquaintances but Leighton (qv) was to prove a more lasting influence. In 1858-9 Prinsep worked with William Morris, J H Pollen (qv) and others on the project to decorate the Oxford Union, a botched enterprise, more fiasco than fresco. Prinsep exhibited at the Royal Academy in 1862 and annually thereafter. Accomplished rather than gifted, he was perhaps too versatile in his talents to achieve greatness. With Leighton he was a keen member of the volunteer movement, serving as an officer in the Artists' Rifles. In 1877 Prinsep went to India to paint Lord Lytton's durbar for the proclamation of Victoria as Empress of India and on his return published *Imperial India : An Artist's Journal*. He had two plays staged and published two novels. Handsome, powerfully built and effortlessly charming, in 1884 Prinsep married money and was never under any financial pressure to work thereafter. He died at Holland Park and is buried in a suitably flamboyant pseudo-medieval tomb in Brompton cemetery. Prinsep's house was converted into flats in 1948.

James Ferrier Pryde

Pryde (1866-1941), a Scot, struggled financially (but succeeded artistically) as a poster artist (Rowntree's cocoa etc.) before finding his niche with melancholy landscapes. Pryde's wife described him as "one of those men who are attractive to women without making any great exertions to be so." Dilatory, unpractical, extravagant but never prolific, Pryde survived his last years at Lansdowne House (qv) on a Civil List pension of £110.

Queen Elizabeth College

Like so many constituent parts of the University of London, Queen Elizabeth College was the outcome of a haphazard evolution. In 1878 King's College organised a course of lectures for women in Kensington's Vestry Hall. The following year the lectures were held in No. 5 Observatory Avenue (later 9 Hornton Street). The initiative proved sufficiently successful to justify the establishment of a Ladies' (later Women's) Department of King's College, London, which opened at 13 Kensington Square in 1885. In 1908 the Department began offering Home Science and Economics courses.

Reconstituted as the Household and Social Science Department of King's College for Women, it re-opened at Campden Hill in 1915, on the

112. *Queen Elizabeth College at 13 Kensington Square, then described as 'King's College Women's Department'.*

site of Bute House (qv), while the other departments were integrated with King's College on its Strand site. During World War One the college opened a communal kitchen. In 1928 the Campden Hill campus became the autonomous King's College of Household and Social Science. The buildings, incorporating the last home of T B Macaulay (qv), were completed in 1930. The main architect was (Sir) Charles Holden, designer of the University of London's Senate House. Under dieting guru Professor John Yudkin the college pioneered the development of nutrition as an academic discipline. It also had strong links with Africa. In 1953 it became Queen Elizabeth College and began to admit men. In 1985 it was amalgamated with King's College and Chelsea College. In 2003-4 the former college building was converted into luxury apartments.

Peter (Perek) Rachman

'Rachmanism', a term coined by the campaigning MP for North Paddington, Ben Parkin, entered the English language as a synonym for exploitative landlordism. Rachman (1920-62) arrived in England as a stateless, penniless refugee in 1946. Born in Eastern Poland, he had served a spell in Siberia and with the Free Polish forces in Italy. Jobs in an East End furniture factory, with a Wardour Street tailor and selling cheap luggage were followed in 1950 by an ascent into entrepreneurship with the collaboration of an ex-colonel. Financed by the savings of a Bayswater prostitute Rachman set up a flat-letting agency for streetwalkers (£5 a week on the books plus £10 cash). By 1956 he had thirty houses in Notting Hill, thirty more in Shepherd's Bush and twenty flats in Maida Vale. From 1957 onwards he bought up decayed properties in North Kensington at an increasing rate, spurred on by the Rent Act of that year. In decontrolling rents the new law sought to encourage more rented property onto the market; Rachman took it as a green light to force out tenants on previously low controlled rents and substitute new and much higher ones. To rid them of unwanted sitting tenants he would initially offer them a modest sum to leave, then discourage them from staying put by moving prostitutes into adjacent properties or overcrowding nearby apartments with new tenants. Tenants resisting such pressures found themselvs harassed by hired thugs like 'Michael X' who would make their lives unbearable by playing all night music, scattering garbage, killing pets etc. If that failed Rachman simply used his bullies to cut off water and electricity, smash the lavatories and take the locks off doors. Most of Rachman's new tenants were Caribbean or Asian immigrants with little option but to pay extortionate rents for the most squalid accommodation. 1-16 Powis Terrace, for example, was bought for £20,000. Rachman installed a Nigerian landlord who had to hand over £300 a week. Built to house no more than two hundred people the block soon housed twelve hundred. Rachman, having accumulated a portfolio of some hundred or more buildings, mostly residential but also including shady 'clubs', lived the life of a high roller, numbering the notorious call-girls Christine Keeler and Mandy Rice-Davies among his mistresses and Dennis Hamilton, husband of film star Diana Dors, as a gambling buddy. In 1959 the Metropolitan Police set up a special squad to investigate the operations of the thirty-plus companies Rachman used to manipulate his property empire. This led to the uncovering of Rachman's sideline in prostitution and resulted in two prosecutions for keeping a brothel. Rachman nevertheless died a millionaire. Thanks to the protection afforded by the libel laws and despite the endeavours of Ben Parkin and the *Kensing-*

113. Margeurite Radclyffe-Hall. Photograph by Howard Coster.

ton News (qv) Rachman's tangled affairs were only fully exposed after his death and as a spin-off from the disgrace of War Minister John Profumo resulting from the latter's involvement with Keeler and Rice-Davies.

Margeurite Radclyffe-Hall

Born into a financially privileged but emotionally deprived background, the girl who was to call herself 'John' and become known to the world as the writer Radclyffe Hall (1880-1943), grew up (1880-1901) at 14 Addison Road until an inheritance enabled her to move out. Despite an education as disorganised as her family life, she managed to produce five volumes of poems which found public acclaim, some being set to music by Coleridge Taylor, whom Stanford *(qv)* considered one of his most naturally gifted pupils. In 1907 'John' met Mabel Batten (*aka* 'Ladye'), a married socialite over twenty years her senior, set up home with her and, under Ladye's influence, became a Roman Catholic. In 1915 John fell in love with Ladye's sculptor cousin, Una Vincenzo, Lady Troubridge. After Ladye's death in 1916, they began living together and pursued a common interest in spiritualism. This was much in vogue in the aftermath of the Great War as bereaved thousands attempted to contact slaughtered loved ones, although in the case of John and Una the object of their quest was Ladye. Turning to novel-writing as 'Radclyffe Hall', John enjoyed such success with her fourth effort, the award-winning *Adam's Breed* (1926) that, while living at 37 Holland Street (1924-9), she was encouraged to compose a thinly-disguised autobiographical account of lesbian passion under the title *The Well of Loneliness*. Reviled by the popular press as a work of moral depravity, it was successfully prosecuted as an obscene libel and not republished in England until 1949. Printed in Paris and bought in huge numbers in the USA, the book was translated into eleven languages and sold over a million copies in the author's lifetime. John was buried beside Ladye in Highgate cemetery.[60]

Dame Marie Rambert

Born Cyvia Myriam Ramberg in Warsaw, she trained in eurhythmics under Emile Jacques-Delcroze in Geneva from 1909 to 1912 and then worked with the Diaghilev Ballet, training the Ballet Russe in eurhythmics and assisting Nijinsky with choreographing *The Rite of Spring*. After marrying the dramatist Ashley Dukes (qv) in 1918 Rambert (1888-1982) studied under Enrico Cecchetti and then turned to teaching, her most distinguished students being (Sir) Frederick Ashton, (Sir) Robert Helpmann and Pearl Argyle, the first English dancer to make a name for herself. Rambert's first ballet school, opened in 1920, was in Bedford Gardens. In 1931 she founded the Ballet Club to become a permanent company with its own home, which it acquired in the Mercury Theatre (qv). In 1934 the company was renamed Ballet Rambert. Dance historian Arthur Haskell recognized the importance of Marie Rambert's contribution as early as 1938 – attributing her creativity to the fact that she was "not a teacher in the ordinary sense of the word but a frustrated dancer who makes others dance in her place." Frustrated or not, she could still turn cartwheels at seventy. Dame Marie Rambert lived at 19 Campden Hill Gardens from 1920 until her death.[61]

William George Rawlinson

Rawlinson (1840-1928) made a fortune out of dyed silks and used it to collect and study the drawings, water colours and engravings of Turner. He also collected Whistler etchings and Chinese porcelain and entertained artistic circles at his Campden Hill residence, Hill Lodge.

Redonda

Redonda is a mile-long volcanic rock in the Leeward Islands. On his fifteenth birthday Matthew Phipps Shiel (1865-1947) was crowned King Felipe of Redonda. Five years later he emigrated to London, lived in St Charles Square and pursued an erratic literary career which brought him into contact with Robert Louis Stevenson, Arthur Machen (qv) and his acolyte and 'successor', Terence Ian Fytton Armstrong (1912-70), who grew up at Colville Gardens and 40 Royal Crescent and became an obsessive jackdaw hoarder of literary memorabilia. Writing as John Gawsworth (a convoluted homage to his supposed descent from Shakespeare's 'Dark Lady'), Armstrong became a poet and bibliographer, compiled an early biography of Machen and successfully campaigned for Shiel to receive a civil list pension. Shiel in return appointed Gawsworth Poet Laureate of Redonda and, with a blood-oath, his successor to its 'throne'. Whereas Shiel had treated the island as pretty much a private fantasy Gawsworth shrewdly exploited its potential for his own literary self-promotion as Juan I. (By 1938 he had already become the youngest Fellow of the Royal Society of Literature). Treating the Alma pub at 175 Westbourne Grove as the setting for his 'Court-in-exile', he 'ennobled' Arthur Machen, Victor

Gollancz *(qqv)*, Arthur Ransome, Rebecca West and others with titles in recognition of services to Shiel or Redonda. Gawsworth managed to found two literary magazines, kick-started Lawrence Durrell's literary career, churned out his own neo-Georgian verse and indulged his enthusiasms for Jacobitism, the IRA, and Indian nationalism. After wartime service in the RAF and an able period as editor of *Poetry Review*, he descended into alcoholism, living off the sale of literary detritus at 35 Sutherland Place. In 1970 BBC's *Late Night Line-Up* attempted to rescue him from indigence with a documentary tribute-cum-appeal. Gawsworth blew most of the resulting £1,400 on a mammoth binge in the Alma and a trip to Florence, dying in the Brompton hospital later that year. Gawsworth's literary executor Jon Wynne-Tyson assumed the title of Juan II, abdicating in 1997 in favour of the eminent Spanish novelist Javier Marias, who has honoured A S Byatt ('Duchess of Morpho Eugenia') and William Boyd (Duke of Brazzaville) and founded an imprint dedicated to Redondan writers.[62]

Zandra Rhodes

Eccentric fashion designer Zandra Rhodes (1940-) bought a large house in Notting Hill in the 1970s and eventually sold it to fund The Fashion and Textile Museum which she opened in Bermondsey in 2003.[63]

114. 8 Addison Road, built by Halsey Ricardo.

Halsey Ralph Ricardo

The apartments now numbered 55 and 57 (originally 15 and 17) Melbury Road were originally semi-detached houses built in 1894 by Halsey Ricardo (1854-1928) for Sir Alexander Rendel (1829-1918), designer of the Royal Albert Dock and consulting engineer to the Indian State Railways. The hall of No. 55, which was Rendel's home, features lush peacock-blue tiles by William de Morgan. No. 57 was taken by Sir Ernest Debenham, a wealthy businessman and cousin of Neville Chamberlain. Debenham was so impressed by Ricardo's work that he commissioned him to build No. 8 Addison Road. This fantastical Arts and Crafts confection, also featuring de Morgan tiles, was built in 1905-8 and took up the sites of three previous houses. Ricardo was a fervent partisan of structural polychromy and the exterior features blue-grey bricks, glazed terracotta and green and blue glazed bricks. It had a basement gymnasium, a school room, a lift, a garden breakfast room, a 'Motor house' and seventeen bedrooms. The interiors were much used in Joseph Losey's film *Secret Ceremony*, starring Elizabeth Taylor, Mia Farrow, Peggy Ashcroft and Robert Mitchum. At Leighton House *(qv)* Ricardo added the Perrin Gallery, opened in 1929.

'Riots'

Recurrent episodes of inter-racial violence broke out in Nottingham in August 1958 and in Notting Hill a week later that same month. In both cases assaults seem to have occurred initially in reaction to the sight of black men in the company of white women. The media favoured the term 'riots' to describe the sporadic incidents that occurred and the police blamed

96

hooligans, both black and white. The Notting Hill disorders, spread over the period August 20-September 5, in fact consisted of gangs of white working-class youths, armed with iron bars, belts and knives, roaming the streets to attack black men unlucky enough to be caught alone. Window-smashing was a subsidiary activity. Unsurprisingly, black men, many of them ex-servicemen, organised in their own defence. Of 108 persons charged with affray, possessing offensive weapons etc. 72 were white and 36 'coloured'. Nine white men were finally charged and sentenced to four years for violent offences. While some homes, shops and pubs offered refuge to actual or potential victims of what a judge called a "minute and insignificant section of the population", many residents simply held aloof, expressing silent resentment at the alleged impact of the newcomers on the local housing problem, the annoyance caused by loud parties and the involvement of at least some black men in the sleazy and vicious exploitation associated with the notorious landlord, Peter Rachman (*qv*). The 'riots' provide the background for Colin MacInnes' (*qv*) novel *Absolute Beginners*. The subsequent murder of Kelso Cochrane (*qv*) and the efforts of Sir Oswald Mosley (*qv*) to exploit racial tension galvanised local residents to support a range of positive initiatives such as carnival (*qv*) and the Notting Hill Social Council, formed at the instigation of the Meth-odist church in Lancaster Road as an umbrella organisation to promote the efforts of community leaders.[64]

The Roberts

Robert Colquhon (1914-62) and Robert MacBryde (1913-66), *aka* 'The Roberts', both from Ayrshire, became lovers as fellow students at the Glasgow School of Art, held their first joint exhibition at Kilmarnock, Colquhon's birthplace, in 1938 and were inseparable thereafter, although apt to quarrel violently when drunk. Colquhon, tall, thin and taciturn, was complemented by his wiry, energetic, uninhibitedly kilted partner. They settled at 77 Bedford Gardens in 1941 after Colquhon was invalided out of the RAMC with heart trouble, MacBryde being exempted from service by a tubercular condition. Colquhon continued to drive ambulances as a civilian, painting by night. *The Listener* hailed his pictures. Wyndham Lewis likewise hailed and also praised MacBryde's wit. Other visitors to their domain included Francis Bacon, Lucian Freud, Rodrigo Moynihan and Dylan Thomas. John Minton shared the house for a short time. In 1942 the Polish artist Jankel Adler (1895-1949) took a studio in their house and became MacBryde's artistic mentor. In 1946 another artist, Ronald Searle (1920-), moved in; he subsequently became a celebrated caricaturist, illustrator, animator and designer of commemorative medallions. Searle, recovering from three years internment by the Japanese in Singapore's notorious Changi gaol, was unlikely to disturb the domestic harmony of Bedford Gardens. Harmony was, however, so disturbed by what the landlord called 'drunken orgies' that in 1947 the Roberts were evicted and never established a permanent home again. Disoriented, they entered a downward spiral of drinking, diminished creativity and shrinking acclaim, returning to take rooms at 9 Westbourne Terrace and 8 Norland Square in 1958-9. Colquhon died in MacBryde's arms. MacBryde moved to Dublin and was killed by a car on his way home from a pub.

(Walford) Graham Robertson

Robertson (1866-1948) was an artist, an illustrator, a costume designer and a dramatist, wealthy enough to be a dabbler, a friend of Henry James and Sarah Bernhardt and the subject of one of John Singer Sargent's most celebrated portraits. Painted in 1894 and now in the Tate Gallery, the picture depicts Robertson full length, wearing a long overcoat of superb cut (indoors), holding a jade-handled cane and with his feet insouciantly crossed, with a large dog lying beside him. In his autobiography, *Time Was*, Robertson recorded sardonically that the painting had made him "a Notable Personage ... it was a second-hand notability, a reflected aureole but distinctly noticeable." Robertson added that, as an obliging model, he had had his hands painted by Poynter (*qv*) and had been used by Crane (*qv*) for "immortals of uncertain shape and sex" but Sargent was the first to want to paint all of him as he was, though even then Robertson suspected that what really attracted the artist were the overcoat and the dog.

Robertson had studied art at South Kensington but preferred on the whole to collect it rather than create it. When asked why he had never painted a self-portrait he riposted immediately "because I am not my style". Robertson's house at 47 (then 13) Melbury Road was built in 1892-3 but used as a studio and setting for receptions while its owner actually lived at 9 Argyll Road. From 1896 until his early death from typhoid in 1904 the studio was shared by the gifted Scottish water-colour painter Arthur Melville (1855/8-1904), who specialised in Spanish and Orientalist subjects. The house was converted to flats in 1948.

Revd. Arthur Dalgarno Robinson

Previously curate of St Stephen's, Shepherd's Bush, Robinson (d. 1899) moved to Notting Dale in 1860 and worked there until his death. For his first seven years he served without pay and bought at his own expense a site for St Clement's church, which was built to the designs of James Piers St Aubyn, consecrated in 1867 and completed in 1869. A site had been promised by local landowner James Whitchurch but failed to materialise. Lord Leverhulme did later present the church with a large cartoon of Jesus at the well of Samaria by Burne-Jones.

Robinson gave equal priority to establishing one of the first (1866) schools for the children of the Potteries (*qv*). In 1875 he began building a second set of schools. Following the division St Clement's parish in 1881, Robinson threw himself into fund-raising for the new parish church of St Helen's, built in 1881-4 to the designs of H Currey. The site, on St Quintin's Avenue, was close to that of the now vanished Notting Barns farmhouse. Robinson also built a sixteen room vicarage, surrounded by a garden and fruit trees. Robinson's devotion is commemorated in the names of Dalgarno Gardens and Dalgarno Way. St Helen's was destroyed in World War Two and replaced by the present building of 1954-6 which contains an organ case and stained glass by Ninian Comper. The pews, designed by R Norman Shaw (*qv*), were originally from the Harrow Mission church of Holy Trinity, Latimer Road.

Rock and Pop

In 1965 Tom Jones's manager Gordon Mills co-wrote *It's Not Unusual* in his council flat in Campden Hill Towers. Sandie Shaw turned it down, leaving it to launch Tom Jones' career.

In 1966 Pink Floyd played in the hall of All Saints' church (*qv*), Powis Gardens as part of the London Free School's Light and Sound workshops. As a result of seeing the group play here EMI offered them a contract. Hawkwind, then known as Group X, played their first concert in the hall and were signed up for a recording contract on the recommendation of the late John Peel who was in the audience. They named their album Mountain Grill after a Portobello Road cafe.

In 1967 Marc Bolan lived at 57 Blenheim Crescent when forming T Rex and wrote *Ride a White Swan* there.

In 1970 Jimi Hendrix took what proved to be a fatal overdose in the basement of the Samarkand Hotel at 21-22 Lansdowne Crescent. His actual death occurred in the Cumberland Hotel at Marble Arch the following day.

In 1970 Led Zeppelin recorded the electronic section and wrote the lyrics of *Stairway to Heaven* and other parts of Led Zeppelin IV at Sarm Studios West at 8 Basing Street. In 1984 Frankie Goes To Hollywood recorded their first LP *Welcome to The Pleasure Dome* at Sarm Studios. In the same year Band Aid recorded the most famous charity record ever there – *Do They Know Its Christmas*? George Michael recorded *Older at Sarm* in 1995.

In 1973 Supertramp used 35 Holland Villas Road as a collective home and it was there that they wrote the hit single *Breakfast in America* and material for their first hit album *Crime of the Century*.

In the 1970s Annie Lennox served behind the counter at Mr Christian's delicatessen in

Elgin Crescent.

In 1989 Bill Wyman of the Rolling Stones opened his restaurant Sticky Fingers at 1a Phillimore Gardens. An *Evening Standard* survey rated its hamburgers the best in London.

In 1990 Damon Albarn, Blur's singer, was a barman at the Portobello Hotel, 22 Stanley Gardens. The hotel has been used by Mick Jagger, Sting, George Michael, Kate Moss, Johnny Depp and Oasis. Tina Turner at one time lived in the house next door.

In 1996 Paul Weller lived at 2 Woodsford Square after the break-up of The Style Council.

Jarvis Cocker of Pulp lives in Ladbroke Grove. Other local residents at the time of writing include Robbie Williams, Damon Albarn and Will Young.

The group All Saints took their name from the recording studios in that road.

St Andrew and St Philip, Golborne Road

Erected in 1869-70 to the designs of E Bassett Keeling and demolished after its benefice was united with that of St Thomas, Kensal Road in 1951.

St Barnabas, Addison Road

Built in 1827-9 to the designs of Lewis Vulliamy *(qv)* on a soggy site donated by Lord Holland, St Barnabas became a parish church in its own right in 1856.

Tudor Gothic in style, it is Georgian in shape, planned with the sermon rather than the sacrament as the central

115. *The spectacular roof of St Clement's, Treadgold Street.*

feature of worship. The church was altered in 1860-1, 1885-7, 1895-6, 1909 and 1957-8. In 1864 the painter G F Watts *(qv)* married actress Ellen Terry here. Byam Shaw *(qv)*, whose own monument here is Gothic, designed the Arts and Crafts stained glass window depicting SS Cecilia and Margaret.

St Clement, Treadgold Street

Designed by James Piers St Aubyn (1815-95) and built in 1867-9 for the poor of Notting Dale, the church has lost its original polychrome interior to layers of whitewash but remains dominated by its complex roof-ribbing supported on slender cast-iron columns. The church is now amalgamated with St Mark and St James Norlands.

St Columb, Lancaster Road

Built in 1900-1. The church was sold to the Serbian community in 1952 and rededicated to St Sava. There is a bronze memorial tablet to Serb resistance

116. *St Francis of Assisi.*

leader Drazha Mihailovich (1893-1946).

St Francis of Assisi, Pottery Lane

The site for this church was acquired by the English branch of the Oblates of St Charles Borromeo. The building was paid for by an Oblate, Father Rawes. Designed by Henry Clutton (1819-93), a Catholic convert, its construction (1859-60) was supervised by John Francis Bentley, future architect of Westminster Cathedral. Bentley also designed the magnificent alabaster high altar and reredos, the ingenious Lady Chapel, the porch and very fittingly the baptistry, as he was the first person to be baptised in the church, following his conversion in 1862. Bentley also designed the candlesticks, monstrance, vestments and many of the fittings. The paintings on slate of the Seven Dolours of Our Lady and Stations of the Cross were done by N H J Westlake *(qv)*,

117. The eccentric St George's, Aubrey Walk.

who collaborated with Bentley on the stained-glass of the east windows.

St George's, Aubrey Walk

Built to the eccentric (according to Pevsner 'atrocious') designs of Enoch Bassett Keeling (1837-86) in 1864-65, its originally flamboyant interior has been severely toned down and much altered. *The Building News* called the style "continental Gothic, freely treated". The *Survey of London* opts for "strange and wilful". St George's was built at the expense (£9,000) of builder John Bennett (1805-80) of Westbourne Park Villas to provide a living for his son, George, the first incumbent. During the 1990s the church underwent substantial refurbishment and has since expanded its regular congregation.[65]

St Helen, St Helen's Gardens

The original church of 1884 was bombed and replaced in 1954-6. Features include pews by R Norman Shaw *(qv)* and an organ case and stained glass by Ninian Comper.

St James Norlands, St James's Gardens

Built in white brick in 1844-5 to the designs of Lewis Vulliamy, this Grade II listed structure originally featured polychrome interior decoration, removed in 1950. The church featured briefly in the film *Notting Hill*. Fund-raisers made marketing history by raising £150,000 towards restoration costs from a single superbly tailored mail-shot, 90% of the donors never having given to the church before. St James's provides the venue for performances by the W11 Opera company for Young People.[66]

118. St James Norlands, as it was eventually built, minus a spire, designed by Vulliamy.

119. A plaque commemorating the first stone of St James's Square, now St James's Gardens.

St John the Baptist, Holland Road

Building this church began in 1874 but it was not consecrated until 1889 and not finished until 1911, the final outcome bearing only a par-

120. *The proposed church and square, at that time to be called St James's Square, prepared by the architect John Barnett.*

tial relationship to the original scheme devised by James Brooks (1825-1901), mixing Burgundian Gothic and English Cistercian.

St John the Evangelist, Ladbroke Grove

Built in 1844-45 to the designs of John Hargrave Stevens (died 1875) and George Alexander, St John's holds a commanding site, at the summit of Notting Hill, where the grandstand of the abortive Hippodrome (*qv*) race course once stood and serves as the central pivot for the whole Ladbroke estate (*qv*) planning scheme. Pevsner observed that the church was "architecturally undistinguished, although far more

archaeologically correct (that is, at the time, 'modern') than for example St James Norlands." Professor James Stevens Curl observes that the tower and spire are based on those of the church of St Mary at Witney and remarks acerbically of the Kentish ragstone used in construction that it is "representative of that early phase of Gothic Revival church building in which an inappropriately rural material was used." (Despite such carping the building is still listed as Grade II). The reredos (1890) was designed by Sir Aston Webb (*qv*). In 2001 a major cleaning of the church and repair of the spire were undertaken at a cost of £250,000.

From 1853 to 1857 the organ-

ist at St John's was the composer Charles Edward Horsley (1822-76).

St Mark, St Mark's Road

C H Blake, developer of the Ladbroke estate (*qv*) gave the site. E Bassett Keeling provided the design, which The *Building News* denounced as "an atrocious specimen of coxcombry". It was consecrated in 1863.

St Mary Abbots

The original parish church of Kensington, it takes its name from having come into the possession of the Abbey of Abingdon *c*.1100. Rebuilt between 1683 and 1696 and with its western tower con-

123. St Mark's church, St Mark's Road.

structed in 1770-2, it was declared unsafe in 1866. The present building, designed by Sir George Gilbert Scott, designer of the Albert Memorial, dates from 1868-72. The spire was completed in 1879 and the cloister added in 1889-93.[67]

St Mary's RC Chapel, Holland Street

This was the first place built in Kensington specifically for Catholic worship since the Reformation. The promoter was Richard Gillow of Bute House (*qv*). It acquired a charity school in 1830 and parochial status in 1850. In 1869 it became entirely a school, demolished *c*.1904.

St Michael and All Angels, Ladbroke Road

Built 1870-1 by James Edmeston Jnr. and his son J S Edmeston in "Rhineland Romanesque". The southwest tower was never completed. The church was paid for by the father of the first

121. Interior of St John the Baptist, Holland Road, designed by James Brooks.

122. The old St Mary Abbots church, looking west. From a print published in 1824.

incumbent (from 1871 to 1886) Edward Ker Gray, who made it famous for its music (the then Duke of Edinburgh played the violin in the church orchestra) and attracted a fashionable congregation, including members of the Royal Family. The congregation declined socially with the area following Gray's departure for Mayfair. The church's original murals were painted over in 1955.

St Peter, Kensington Park Road

By the time the Ladbroke estate was developed the classical style of this church (consecrated 1857) by Thomas Allom (qv) was long out of fashion. The Italian Renaissance chancel was added in 1879 and further embellishments of mosaic and alabaster were added in the 1880s, testimony to the affluence of the parish. The site was donated by the developer C H Blake. The church nowadays serves as a regular venue for the Kensington Chamber orchestra.

St Quintin Estate

In 1859 Yorkshireman Col. Matthew Chitty Downes St Quintin of the 17th Lancers inherited Notting Barns Farm, which extended over some 150 acres. The farmhouse stood at what is now the corner of St Quintin Avenue and Chesterton Road. The colonel, an absentee, was content to let others do the developing from 1864 onwards. Between 1871 and 1890 over four hundred houses were put up. Patches

124. St Peter's in Kensington Park Road.

of open land remained, however, until the 1920s and were used for cricket, tennis, athletics, grazing and the annual Notting Hill Flower and Home Improvement Show.

St Thomas, Kensal Road

Romaine and Brierley's original church of 1889 was destroyed in World War Two and replaced by a 1967 building by Romilly Craze.

St Volodymyr

Unveiled in 1988 to commemorate the thousandth anniversary of the saint's role in Christianising the Ukraine, this statue on Holland Park Avenue commemorates the king who ruled the Ukraine from 980 to 1015. The sculptor was Winnipeg-based Ukrainian-Canadian Leonard/ Leonid Molodozhanyn (1915-) *aka* Leo Mol. Other copies of the work are to be found in Winnipeg, Saskatoon, Toronto and the Vatican.

Linley Sambourne ... and his house

Edward Linley Sambourne (1844-1910) abandoned his engineering apprenticeship to cartoon for *Punch* for forty-three years, eventually succeeding Sir John Tenniel as cartoonist-in-chief. Sambourne also illustrated travel books and an edition of *The Water Babies*. A passionate photographer who did his developing in the bath, he joined the Camera Club in 1893 and used many of his pictures as the basis for cartoons, having his family and servants pose as figures from history or current politics.(His personal predilection was for female nudes.) Almost 15,000 of his photographs and 1,000 products of his pencil survive. Sambourne's marital home from 1874, at 18 Stafford Terrace, is a virtual time-capsule of bourgeois comfort and rather eclectic 'artistic' taste – the William Morris wallpapers are original, as are paintings by Luke Fildes (qv), a family friend. Other friends included the artists Watts, Crane (qqv) and George du Maurier, the writers Rider Haggard and Bret Harte and librettist W S Gilbert (qv). Linley Sambourne House very appropriately served as the first headquarters of the Victorian Society. This was not simply because it is what it is but because it was also the Society's birthplace. After the Sambournes' deaths No. 18 passed to their son Roy who left it virtually unaltered until his death, unmarried, in 1946. It then passed to his sister Maud Messel, whose daughter Anne (mother of the future Lord Snowdon) used it as a pied-à-terre and gave parties there. At a Guy Fawkes celebration in 1957 she proposed forming a society to campaign for what was then regarded as the hideously unaccceptable art and architecture of the Victorian period and enlisted the enthuasistic support of Sir John Betjeman and Professor Nikolaus Pevsner. The property was acquired by the Greater London Council in 1980 and, after its abolition in 1986, passed to the Royal Borough of Kensington and Chelsea. Shirley Nicholson has used the diaries kept by Sambourne's wife, Marion, to produce a detailed study of the family's domestic life, *A Victorian Household* (Sutton Publishing 2000).[68]

Eugene Sandow (1867-1925)

Born Friedrich Wilhelm Mueller in Konigsberg, East Prussia, the pioneer of body-building ran away to join the circus, adopting the stage-name Eugene Sandow (1867-1925). Developing his physique through systematic weight-training, Sandow achieved early fame in London in 1889 when he defeated the stage strongman 'Sampson' in a contest of strength. In 1893 Thomas Edison captured 'The Modern Hercules' on film and in the same year youthful impresario Florenz Ziegfeld hired Sandow to perform at the World's Colombian Exposition in Chicago and then became his manager. Thanks to Ziegfeld Sandow made prolific and

skilful use of photography to boost his image and career. Books followed, such as *Strength and How to Obtain It* (1897). After touring the world with vaudeville companies Sandow settled in London to open a 'Physical Culture Studio'. Its elegant panelling, potted palms and Persian carpets banished the image of the sweaty gymnasium, enabling it to appeal to the respectable and affluent classes.

By 1905 Sandow's studio had become a chain and a keen business sense enabled him to market not only courses of instruction and gymnastic equipment but a wide range of associated products, ranging from corsets to cocoa. When London hosted the fourth Olympiad in 1908 an appeal for funds raised £15,000 from individual donors – including £1,500 from Sandow, the largest sum by far donated by a single person. In 1909 Sandow proved his loyalty to his adopted country by offering to provide free physical training for would-be recruits to the newly-established Territorial Army. In 1911 the 'Mighty Monarch of Muscle' was appointed special instructor in physical culture to King George V. By 1907 Sandow had become wealthy enough to move into 16 Holland Park Avenue where "the world's strongest man" lived until his death, probably from syphilis. He was buried in Putney Vale Cemetery – at the request of his family, in an unmarked grave. Within a month Sandow's wife and daughters

125. *Siegfried Sassoon.*

had sold off the family home and its contents and left London for good.[69]

Siegfried Sassoon

Sassoon (1886-1967) occupied 23 Campden Hill Square from 1925 until 1932 and was already no stranger to the area, knowing Robert Ross and being a nephew of Hamo Thornycroft *(qv)*. During this period Sassoon published three volumes of verse and the semi-autobiographical *Memoirs of a Fox-Hunting Man* (1928) and *Memoirs of an Infantry Officer* (1930), which in effect recounted his own transformation from dilettante poetaster to author of substance and a hero (Sassoon won the MC and was recommended for a VC). Sassoon had always been searching for the divine spark of true inspiration and found it in real gunfire. By this period, too, the power of Sassoon's war poems, initially too shocking for public acceptance, was beginning to be appreciated, while the writer himself was moving towards the spiritual preoccupations which were eventually to lead him into Catholicism. Sassoon's marriage in 1933 prompted him to leave London for Wiltshire where he spent the rest of his life. His portrait by Glyn Philpot *(qv)* is in the Fitzwilliam Museum.[70]

Sam Selvon (1923-94)

Notting Hill and Bayswater figure frequently as settings in the novels of Samuel Dickson Selvon (1923-94), who arrived from his native Trinidad in 1950. Of Indian descent, Selvon lived at numerous rundown West London addresses and, initially supporting himself by menial work, lived the sort of life commonly experienced by many of the poorer Caribbean immigrants whose stories he would retail in a series of episodic sketches as *The Lonely Londoners* (1956), the first Caribbean novel to be written totally in dialect. *Moses Ascending* (1975) although published after Selvon had emigrated to Canada, satirises the Black Power activists of North Kensington.

Charles Haslewood Shannon and Charles de Sousy Ricketts

Ricketts (1866-1931), sixteen, diminutive, dynamic and witty, and Shannon (1863-1937), nineteen, tall, blond and ruddy, met at the City and Guilds Technical Art School in Lambeth and became artistic and domestic partners for the rest of their lives – nicknamed Marigold and Orchid by Oscar Wilde. Together they initially undertook fine book production, designing Wilde's major works, edited five issues of an avant-garde art journal, *The Dial* (1889-97) and exhibited jointly in Manchester and New York. Aesthetically Shannon was a follower of Watts *(qv)*, Ricketts of Rossetti. Neither was drawn towards more contemporary mentors. Moving into Lansdowne House *(qv)*, which was to be their home until 1923, they entertained a wide artistic acquaintance including Roger Fry, William Rothenstein, Max Beerbohm and Charles Conder, as well as Diaghilev, Nijinsky, Bakst, Yeats and Shaw – who described Ricketts as one of life's natural aristocrats. Despite their relative poverty, never earning more than £1,000 a year between them, Ricketts and Shannon collected art eclectically but astutely. (In 1908 Ricketts bought, for 35 shillings in Bayswater, a medallion by Masaccio which he presented to the National Gallery.) Over decades they acquired Hokusai prints, old master drawings, gemstones and Egyptian and Greek antiquities to the eventual value of £40,000.

Ricketts turned to painting, sculpture and designing jewellery and in 1915 turned down the directorship of the National Gallery. He was eventually (1928) elected RA but found his true metier in stage design, notably for the premiere of Shaw's *Saint Joan* (1924) and the 1926 D'Oyly Carte production of *The Mikado*. From that year until his death he was art adviser to the National Gallery of Canada.

Shannon also turned from wood-engraving, their original shared skill, made redundant by photo-gravure, to painting and lithography. Elected RA in 1921, Shannon nearly died from a grave injury to the head after falling from a ladder in 1929 while rehanging one of his own works, returned from loan. Ricketts sold his collection of Persian miniatures for £4,000 to pay for nursing care but Shannon remained tragically oblivious to all until his death. Their collections were bequeathed to the British Museum and the Fitzwilliam Museum in Cambridge. Their portraits hang side by side in the National Portrait Gallery.

Sir James Jebusa Shannon

Born in New York of Irish parentage, Shannon (1862-1923) came to London at sixteen, intending only to train. After studying under Poynter *(qv)* at South Kensington, Shannon swiftly prospered as a society portraitist, prompting a contemporary observation of him as "among the foremost exponents of this branch of art and ... without exception the most dashing ... he has painted more lovely women than any portrait artist in the same space of time." President of the Royal Society of Portrait Painters in 1910, he was knighted the year before his death. Shannon lived at 10-10a Holland Park Road (then No. 3, 'South House'), a house and studio built for him in 1892-3. The residential part was the adapted farmhouse of Holland Farm (which had been rebuilt in 1859), with the exterior altered to match the new studio built to the east The two parts were divided after Shannon's death.

Richard Norman Shaw

Norman Shaw (1831-1912) is best known for such prominent London landmarks as New Scotland Yard, the Piccadilly (now Le Meridien) Hotel and Albert Hall Mansions. But he also worked on a more domestic (if still lavish) scale, notable examples being in Melbury Road where he designed homes for Sir Luke Fildes and Marcus Stone (*qqv*) and West House for George Boughton (*qv*). Shaw's association with the art world owed much to John Callcott Horsley RA (*qv*), whose patronage led to many other commissions by Royal Academicians. Shaw's *DNB* entry proclaims magniloquently of his achievement "the style was called 'Queen Anne'; but in Shaw's work it was not a revival of the eighteenth century so much as a recovery of the building art."

Stafford Terrace

Stafford Terrace was built between 1868 and 1874 by builder Joseph Gordon Davis. The Italianate design resembles similar houses he built in Pimlico. No. 12 was the home of Freddie Mercury in the 1980s. No. 18 belonged to

126. *Richard Norman Shaw.*

Linley Sambourne (*qv*), who paid £2,000 for an 89-year lease.

Stage Struck

The actress known as Madame Vestris (1797-1856) graduated from opera (contralto) to acting to becoming London's first female theatre manager. She was deserted by her first husband, a bankrupt French ballet-dancer and saved herself through her understanding of stagecraft, to which she contributed much. Mme Vestris lived at 2 Elm Place, with her second husband the actor Charles James Mathews, in a house of 1790 which later became the Kensington Institute for the Blind.

Ranging from Shakespeare to farce, the professional career of Alfred Wigan (1814-78) lasted almost forty years and included a command performance before the Queen at Windsor and stints as manager of the Olympia

127. *Madame Vestris.*

Theatre and the Princess's Theatre. Something of a French scholar, Wigan excelled in the role of Frenchmen speaking broken English. Wigan's wife, Leonora (1805-80) began as a rope-dancer and stilt walker before graduating to the stage, often playing opposite her husband. In the 1870s the couple were living at Little Campden House (*qv*).

Music hall superstar Albert Chevalier (1861-1923) was born at 17 (then 21) St Ann's Villas, Royal Crescent. Educated at Clanricarde College, Bayswater, he was already taking part in 'penny readings' at the Cornwall Hall, Cornwall Road by the age of eight. At 14 he joined the Roscius Dramatic Club which put on amateur productions at the Ladbroke Hall. Making his first professional appearance at fifteen Chevalier served an apprenticeship of fourteen years on the 'legitimate' stage before shocking fellow thespians by becoming the hit of the 1890s with coster songs of his own composition, such as *Knocked 'em in the Old Kent Road* and *My Old Dutch*. In all Chevalier wrote eighty songs and nearly twenty plays and owed his great success to the wit and polish which made him, in the title of one of his own songs, *Funny Without Being Vulgar*.

Theatrical impresario Charles Hayden Coffin (1862-1922) lived in Bedford Gardens for nearly thirty years until his death.

Comedian (John) Robertson Hare (1891-1979) lived in Holland Park Avenue in the 1930s, having made his name in Ben Travers' Aldwych farces of the previous decade, such as *Rookery Nook* (1926). He enjoyed a second bout of stardom late in life thanks to the television series *All Gas and Gaiters*.

Sir Charles Villiers Stanford

A hugely prolific composer, Stanford (1854-1924) is nowadays remembered rather as a teacher. Irish-born and initially trained in music by Irishmen, he read classics at Cambridge, becoming organist of Trinity College while still an undergraduate. Taken up by Tennyson and the Gloucester and Birmingham Festivals, Stanford settled in London in 1892 and from 1894 until 1916 lived at 56 Hornton Street. Stanford's chamber music, seven operas and seven symphonies failed to achieve the success accorded to his 'Irish Rhapsodies', sea songs, church anthems and

large-scale choral works such as his *Requiem* (1897) and *Stabat Mater* (1907). He served as conductor of the Cambridge University Music Society and director of the London Bach Choir and Leeds Festival. Stanford was also the first professor at the Royal College of Music and from 1887 professor of music at Cambridge as well, holding both posts until the year of his death. Stanford's pupils are a roll of honour in English music, including Coleridge Taylor, Holst, Vaughan Williams, Ireland and Bliss. Stanford's ashes were honoured with burial in Westminster Abbey in recognition of his major contribution to the revival of church music.

Howard Staunton

A blue plaque on No. 117 Lansdowne Crescent marks the former home of the man who wasn't quite world chess champion. A Shakespeare scholar and possibly at some point an actor, Staunton (1810-74) in 1843 beat St Amant of France but lost to Adolf Andersen and simply refused to play Paul Morphy. In 1851 Staunton organised the first ever international chess tournament. He also founded the *Chess Player's Chronicle* as the first magazine devoted to chess and served as chess columnist for the *Illustrated London News*. The standard chess set now used by professionals, designed by Nathaniel Cook, was named in Staunton's honour. In 1997 a memorial stone in the shape of a chess knight was raised over Staunton's previously unmarked grave in Kensal Green cemetery.

Marcus Stone

The son of Royal Academician Frank Stone, Marcus Stone (1840-1921) first exhib-

128. Marcus Stone's house at 8 Melbury Road.

ited at the Royal Academy when he was just eighteen. The death of his father the following year prompted Stone to support himself by providing illustrations for Dickens, notably for *Our Mutual Friend*, and also for the novels of Trollope. Stone became a Dickens' protégé and his frequent house guest. Meanwhile he built his painterly reputation with a series of canvases on historical and literary themes. Elected RA in 1887, Stone then turned to sentimental genre scenes, featuring pensive maidens, flirtatious couples or tense threesomes, often in a Regency period setting. Many will be dimly familiar even now through being reproduced as greetings-cards and table mats more than a century after their composition. A plush studio house at No. 8 Melbury Road was built for Stone in 1875 by R Norman Shaw (*qv*), an indicator of how greatly Stone was already prospering by then. (It was converted into flats *c*.1950.)

George Johnstone Stoney

A professional astronomer before he became a university administrator, Stoney (1826-1911) made important contributions to optics, molecular physics and the study of gases. Stoney also coined the word 'electron'. He settled at 30 Chepstow Crescent in 1893 so that his daughters could have the university education then denied them in his native Ireland.

129. *John McDouall Stuart's house at 9 Campden Hill Square.*

Stormont House

Built as an elegant gated residence in 1786, Stormont House had become a girls' boarding school by 1808 and lost whatever cachet it might have had when seventy slum houses were jammed into the land at its rear, the residents keeping scores of pigs. Evening classes for working men were held in Stormont House in the 1850s and in 1860 a Ragged school was opened there. The area was redeveloped when the lease ran out in 1867. The site of Stormont House is now covered by 1 Clanricarde Gardens

John McDouall Stuart

Born in Dysart, Kirkcaldy, Scotland, Stuart (1815-66) emigrated to Australia in 1838, worked as a surveyor and led six hazardous expeditions into the outback, the last of which gained him a

130. *The Spanish and Portuguese Synagogue in St James's Gardens.*

premium of £2,000 for becoming the first to cross Australia from south to north and back. He was also given a thousand square miles of land. Broken in health and nearly blinded, Stuart was advised to return to England and settled at No. 9 Campden Hill Square (*qv*) in 1864. The Royal Geographical Society acknowledged his achievement with the gift of a watch and a gold medal. Stuart died less than two years after his return. There is a museum dedicated to his memory in his birthplace.[71]

Synagogues

Notting Hill Synagogue, 208 Kensington Park Road was opened in 1900 in a former church hall. A Jewish Lads' Club opened next door in 1904. The size of the local Jewish community peaked in the inter-war period but declined with out-migration to North London. In September 2000 the synagogue closed after a century in existence. The still surviving Spanish and Portuguese Synagogue in St James's Gardens was built in 1928.

131. Syracuse University in Kensington Park Gardens.

Syracuse University

Syracuse University, founded in 1870, has its main campus in upper New York State. Beginning in the 1920s in China, it has been a pioneer in the field of 'study abroad' programmes. Its London campus was initially located in Monmouth Road, off Westbourne Grove, but for a quarter of a century has been based at 24 Kensington Park Gardens in the former home of Calcutta merchant Charles Henry Blake, developer of the Ladbroke estate *(qv)*. The Syracuse programme is one of the largest and oldest of seventy-plus American study abroad programmes in the capital, accommodating up to five hundred students per year, a third coming from universities other than Syracuse. Students, normally in their third year, stay for a semester of thirteen weeks and usually take five elective courses, many of which take advantage of the capital's galleries, museums and media resources.

The Tabernacle Arts Centre, Powis Square

The Tabernacle traces its origin to the foundation of a non-sectarian church in 1869. The community orientation of its cultural activities can be seen as an extension or redefinition of the church's original outreach programmes which were based on a ragged school and a soup kitchen. Semi-derelict and threatened with demolition in the 1960s, the church was converted by the council into a community centre and became a focal point for Caribbean residents, developing youth, family and carnival (qv) programmes. Rising real estate values once again brought a threat of demolition in the 1970s, fended off by a Grade II listing. Complete refurbishment was achieved in 1996-8 thanks to a £4.5 million capital grant. Facilities include a theatre, dance studios, an art gallery, café, bars and meeting rooms.

132. The Tabernacle Arts Centre, Powis Square.

Resident organisations include Beat Dis Arts, Mangrove Steel Band and the Mark Elie Dance Foundation.[72]

Thornwood Lodge

Built in 1813, adjacent to Bute House *(qv)*, Thornwood Lodge was occupied by the Marchioness of Hastings (1817-23), the fourth Earl of Glasgow (1824-30) and, from 1867 until his death, the railway engineer Sir John Fowler (1817-98). Fowler's projects include the first railway bridge to cross the Thames in central London, at Pimlico, the Metropolitan and District Lines and the Forth Bridge. Thornwood Lodge was demolished in 1956.

Sir Hamo Thornycroft

William Hamo Thornycroft's parents were both sculptors, as was his maternal grandfather. Trained by his father (sculptor of the Boadicea monument at Westminster Bridge) and at the Royal Academy, Thornycroft (1850-1925) studied Michelangelo's work in Italy and won the Academy's Gold Medal in 1875. Receiving a spate of commissions he was able to commission for himself Nos. 2-4 Melbury Road, which he designed in collaboration with John Belcher, a lifelong friend. (Belcher also built the studio block now known as 2B in 1892, into which Thornycroft moved). No. 4, at the suggestion of G F Watts *(qv)* was taken by Mr and Mrs Russell Barrington. Mrs B had artistic and literary aspirations and jumped at the "delightful opportunity of entering into the highest precincts of art under the most helpful auspices." Mrs Barrington (died 1933) not only wrote biographies of Leighton *(qv)* and Watts *(qv)* and of her brother-in-law Walter Bagehot and edited Bagehot's voluminous *Complete Works* but also led the campaign to preserve Leighton House *(qv)* as a public memorial to its creator. Thornycroft's most prominent London statues include General Gordon (1888 Embankment Gardens) Cromwell (1899 Old Palace Yard), which won the Medal of Honour at the Paris Exposition of 1900, and Gladstone (1905 Aldwych). Elected RA in 1888, he was knighted in 1917.

Thorpe Lodge

Standing adjacent to Airlie Gardens, this bijou house is presumably named in honour of the designer of Holland House and Campden House *(qqv)*. Built by John Tasker between 1809 and 1817 and now the Sixth Form Centre of Holland Park School, Thorpe Lodge was substantially altered by two prominent residents. Painter Henry Tanworth Wells (1828-1903) was trained as a lithographer but soon became a miniaturist, specialising in portraits of women and children, until 1861 when, fearing for his eyesight, he switched to large works in oils, specialising in portraits of the Volunteer Riflemen, either in groups or as individuals. It was a shrewd choice. Fear of invasion by the revived French Empire of Napoleon III made the Volunteer movement a popular patriotic cause, even among artists. Leighton, Val Prinsep and Colin Hunter *(qqv)* were all keen members of the Artists' Rifles. Self-regard and friendly rivalry among units was reflected in a demand for dashing portraits,

133. *Thorpe Lodge, now the Sixth Form Centre of Holland Park School.*

a demand which Wells fulfilled. Elected RA in 1870 Wells then switched to painting presentation portraits of civic-minded aristocrats, bishops and businessmen. His most popular work (1880) was, however, an imagined depiction – entitled 'Victoria Regina' – of the young queen receiving news of her accession from the Archbishop of Canterbury and Lord Chamberlain.

After Wells' death at the Lodge, it passed to Montagu Norman (1871-1950), then but newly returned from the Boer war. Eton, Cambridge, Leipzig, Switzerland and New York had made Norman fluent in French and German and a rising star in the field of finance. Plagued by ill health at school, he had been invalided home after two years in South Africa, but bearing a DSO. Slightly oddly for the son of a director, and grandson of a governor, of the Bank of England, he was also a member of the Art Workers' Guild. Under Norman's direction, and working from his sketches, the interior of Thorpe Lodge was, in Pevsner's words, "totally transformed inside in 1904-13 in the most lavish turn-of-the-century taste" – exotic wood panelling, hand-wrought light fittings, fireplaces with De Morgan tiles, Japanese peacock embroideries, vine-scroll plaster friezes in the barrel-vaulted dining-room and Wells' studio "transformed into a groin-vaulted music room, dominated by a large seventeenth century stone Italian fireplace with the Medici arms." This genu-

flection to the great Italian banking dynasty neatly reflected Norman's own deferred acceptance of family tradition. Elected to the Court of the Bank of England in 1907, he became Governor in 1920. Normally the position was held for a two year term. Norman remained in post until stricken by illness in 1944.

Tor Villa

Tor Villa, later 1 Tor Villas, then 10 Tor Gardens, was built by James Clarke Hook (1819-1907) after his election as ARA in 1850. Hook, who specialised in scenes of coastal life and died worth in excess of £100,000, vacated the house in 1857 in favour of Holman Hunt (qv). In 1865 it was taken over by Alfred William Hunt (1830-96) who lived there until his death. Hunt, a former Oxford don, was a fecund producer of landscapes, particularly in water-colour. His daughter, Violet, became the mistress of Ford Madox Ford (qv).

Tor Villa was destroyed in World War Two.

The Travel Bookshop

Founded in 1979, The Travel Bookshop at 13-15 Blenheim Crescent was featured in the film *Notting Hill (qv)* – though the actual filming was done elsewhere. As far as its stock goes the shop interprets 'travel' in the broadest sense to range far beyond guide books and embrace history, biography and fiction. The shop's website not only features lists of recommendations but also a regular newsletter.[73]

134. *The Travel Bookshop.*

Treachery

Former Cambridge don and art historian Anthony Blunt (1907-83) was recruited to Soviet intelligence in 1937. His first London home at 30 Palace Court was frequented by many members of that Marxisant network of Oxbridge intelligentsia and homosexuals that espionage expert Anthony Glees has dubbed 'the Homintern'.

Blunt's contemporary, Oxford graduate (Sir) Roger Hollis, having been recently recruited to MI5, was living at 18 Elsham Road between 1938 and 1940. From 1943 onwards he lived at 6 Campden Hill Square (qv). Hollis became director-general of MI5 in 1956, retiring in 1965. Repeated investigations dismissed charges that he was in fact a Soviet mole. The frequently botched conduct of operations during his tenure of office imply an extraordinary degree of ineptitude if he was not.

In 1982 Soviet spy Anatoly Zotov, then living at 23

Campden Hill Gardens was ordered by the British authorities to clear out within a week.

In 1983 42 Holland Park was the home of Arkady Gouk, director of the Soviet intelligence network in Britain, when MI5 traitor Michael Bettaney was arrested on the eve of betraying to him full details of British counter-espionage strategy against KGB and GRU operations in the UK. Gouk was expelled. Bettaney got twenty-three years. Gouk's deputy, Oleg Gordievsky, who was actually an MI6 agent, took over his place as resident.

Trellick Tower, 5 Golborne Road W10

Commissioned by the Greater London Council in 1966 and built between 1968 and 1972 to the designs of Hungarian architect Erno Goldfinger RA (1902-87), when it was completed Trellick Tower was the tallest residential building in Europe and has been likened to the bridge of a battleship and a mutant fridge. It is thirty-one storeys and 322 feet high and contains 217 flats with south-west facing balconies to catch the maximum sunlight. Complemented by secondary dwellings ranging from two-room flats to three-storey houses, the totality was conceived as an integrated housing unit, complete with its own central laundry, nursery school, doctor's surgery and old people's club. High-rise building was seen as a swift solution to London's enduring housing crisis in the early

135. *Trellick Tower.*

1960s but by the time the Tower was completed opinion had turned decisively away from this strategy following the disastrous gas explosion which destroyed the Ronan Point tower block in east London, killing five people. Trellick was not 'system built' and is structurally sound but was still Goldfinger's last commission. He was unrepentant. Although he had fled to Britain in 1933, Goldfinger remained a convinced Marxist. James Dunnett, who worked in Goldfinger's office, opined that Trellick Tower represented "Stalin's architecture as it should have been."

In the 1970s the tabloid press vilified the 'Tower of Terror' as a vertical arena for vandalism, graffiti, muggings, rape, arson, heroin, prostitutes, squatters etc. It was said to have inspired J G Ballard's novel *High Rise* (1975) in which technological breakdown is followed by social breakdown as the occupants of different floors wage war on each other. In

Martin Amis' novel *London Fields* (1989) Trellick Tower is the home of Keith Talent – 'a very bad guy'. The Tower also featured in novelist Hanif Kureishi's effort at film directing *London Kills Me* (1991).

There were genuine horror stories. On the 15th floor a 27-year-old woman was dragged from the lift and raped and a depressed young mother jumped to her death. When the lifts failed a pensioner, forced to walk six flights, suffered a fatal heart attack. In 1982 the GLC spent £343,336 on repairs and an entryphone system – to little effect. In the same year skydiver Francis Donellan jumped to his death from the top when his parachute failed to open.

Goldfinger blamed the residents for its debased condition – "they messed them up – disgusting." Residents date the turnaround to October 1984 when they formed a new association, whose unrelenting pressure brought the benefits of cheap overnight electricity, better lifts, a playground, CCTV and, at last, in 1994, a concierge and 24 hour security. In 1998 the Tower was awarded a Grade II* listing and even critics conceded the quality that went into its construction. In 1999 a Channel 4/English Heritage poll rated it 37th among the 50 best modern buildings in Britain. Once reviled for its gigantism, at the time of writing it is regarded as highly desirable, with the few privately owned flats commanding an appropriate price. In Nick Barlay's novel

Crumple Zone (2000), however, the central character, teacher Cee Harper, still maintains the more jaundiced view. Trellick Tower was built on the former Edenham Street, identified by Charles Booth in the 1890s as especially notable for its poverty.

(And, yes, Ian Fleming did borrow Goldfinger's name for his villain).[74]

Turkish Baths

London's first Turkish bath was opened in Bell Street, just off the Edgware Road in 1860. The charge of one shilling enabled it to be used by "artisans, small shopkeepers, policemen", as witnessed by Dr Goolden of St Thomas's Hospital, who endorsed its therapeutic value in the treatment of such complaints as rheumatism and sciatica. By the end of 1860 three more such baths had opened in the capital and by 1861 there were said to be thirty. But just one was to provide free baths for the needy poor. In 1865 Richard Metcalfe set up a 'hydropathic dispensary' in Notting Hill's deprived Potteries area as an adjunct to Mrs Bayley's *(qv)* Ragged Castle and Workman's Hall in Portland Terrace. A subscriber to the maxim that 'cleanliness is next to godliness', Mrs Bayley saw bathing as another weapon in her crusade to convert the great unwashed. Unfortunately her landlord saw it as a fire risk and closed it down in 1866. There was also a short-lived (1895-7) Turkish bath at 11 All Saints Road.[75]

Twentieth Century Theatre, 291 Westbourne Grove

Built in 1863 as the Victoria Hall, it was renamed the Bijou Theatre in 1866. Used by amateurs and touring companies, the Bijou staged the first London production of Oscar Wilde's *Salome* in 1905. A cinema in 1911-18, it was then taken over by actress-manager Lena Ashwell (Lena Margaret Pocock,1872-1957) for her repertory company. She had made her stage debut at the Bijou, with Beerbohm Tree. (So did Laurence Olivier, who lived in Elgin Crescent in the 1920s.) Having become one of the first recipients of the OBE for her initiative in organising twenty-five companies to entertain British troops during the Great War, Ashwell aimed to bring drama to London's suburbs from her Westbourne Grove base, which she renamed the Century Theatre. Inspired by her past association with Henry Irving, who had impressed upon her that the theatre must be a spiritual, rather than merely a commercial, force in the life of the

136. The Twentieth Century Theatre.

nation, Ashwell skilfully enlisted the support of London's mayors to get permission to use town halls and public baths for performances on payment of a merely nominal fee. But she saw her initially successful experiment crushed by a government entertainment tax in 1929 and gave up the stage to write her autobiography *Myself a Player* (1936). Amateur theatrical groups from Harrods and D H Evans then used the theatre. From 1936, renamed the Twentieth Century Theatre, it became a headquarters for the Rudolph Steiner movement and was used to promote Eurhythmy, although it was still also used by the amateur Notting Hill Players. The building also for a time served as the home of the London Opera School. Stripped out in 1963 to become an antique furniture warehouse, it was restored, listed Grade II and now serves as a private venue for corporate events, exhibitions, receptions etc.

Ukrainians

The presence of the statue of St Volodomyr *(qv)* alerts the curious to local connections with Britain's Ukrainian community. The headquarters of the Federation of Ukrainians in Great Britain is at 78 Kensington Park Road while 49 Linden Gardens similarly serves the Association of Ukrainians in Great Britain, the Association of Ukrainian Women in Great Britain and the Association of Ukrainian Former Combatants in Great Britain.

Evelyn Underhill

Evelyn Underhill (1875-1941) studied history and botany at King's College for Women (Queen Elizabeth's College) *(qv)*, of which she later became an honorary Fellow. A woman of widely varied interests – yachting, bookbinding, metalwork, cats, composing humorous verses – Evelyn Underhill came to a serious commitment to Christianity as an adult, visiting the poor, providing spiritual counselling, writing on mysticism, broadcasting and conducting spiritual retreats. Having worked for naval intelligence during the First World War she declared herself a pacifist during the Second. She lived at 50 Campden Hill Square *(qv)* from 1907 to 1939. Underhill's published works, including three novels, run to 39 books and some 350 articles and reviews. Her work and memory are perpetuated by the Evelyn Underhill Association.[76]

Mrs Violet Van der Elst

A sometime inhabitant of The Lodge, Addison Road, Mrs Van der Elst (1882-1966) became nationally renowned as a high-profile campaigner against capital punishment but she was also at various times in her colourful life celebrated as a composer, portraitist, aviatrix, writer of science fiction, hypnotist, pioneer of hydros, failed parliamentary candidate, compulsive litigant and collector of Chinese art and books on witchcraft. When her second husband, Belgian artist John Van der Elst, died

in 1934 she assuaged her grief by keeping him in a lead coffin for a year while attempting to contact him through seances. In 1937 the year in which she published *The Torture Chamber and Other Stories* she bought the fantastical 100-bedroom Harlaxton Manor in Lincolnshire, thereby saving it from demolition. The daughter of a coalporter and a Quaker washerwoman, Mrs Van der Elst had made her own fortune out of beauty products and the first brushless shaving-cream. At one point a millionairess and "the richest woman in Brighton" with three Rolls-Royces and fifteen servants, she died a frail, penniless recluse in a Kentish nursing-home.

Virgin

Sir Richard Branson, founder of the Virgin business empire, once lived at 19 Denbigh Terrace (once also the home of comedian Peter Cook) and it was there that he signed Mike Oldfield's *Tubular Bells* for the Virgin label. Offices for Virgin Records, the core business, were built at Kensal Road in 1988-9. In 2000 Branson (emerging from a Tardis, dressed as Dr Who) opened Virgin's first 'virtual shop' at Notting Hill Gate. Selling CDs and mobile phones over the counter, it also provided computer access for purchasing any other Virgin brand product or service, from travel tickets to electricity. The Virgin group of two hundred companies employs over 25,000 people and has a global turnover exceeding £3 billion.[77]

Vulliamy Family

Justin Vulliamy came from Switzerland to England in 1704 to study clockmaking, married his master's daughter, succeeded to the business at 68 Pall Mall and was appointed clockmaker to the Crown in 1742. His son Benjamin, who in turn succeeded to the business, bought the Notting Hill property which was later developed as the Norland estate (*qv*) and there sank England's first artesian well (*qv*). His son Benjamin Lewis Vulliamy (1780-1854) specialised in church and railway clocks and became an associate of the Institution of Civil Engineers and a Fellow of the Royal Astronomical Society as well as five times Master of the Clockmakers' Company. Benjamin Lewis's younger brother Lewis Vulliamy (1791-1871) trained under Sir Robert Smirke, architect of the British Museum, and at the Royal Academy where he won both silver and gold medals and a travelling scholarship which gave him four years studying in Italy, Greece and Asia Minor. His first major work (1827-8) was the church of St Barnabas, Addison Road (*qv*). Vulliamy also built St James's, Norlands (1844-5) (*qv*). In the judgment of the *Dictionary of National Biography* "as a Gothic architect his early churches prove him to have been far in advance of his contemporaries at a period when Gothic was but little known." Much of Vulliamy's practice was concerned with alterations and additions to existing buildings but he

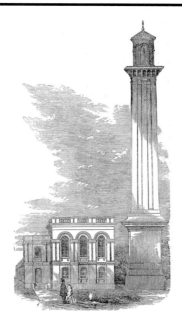

137. The Water Tower of the Grand Junction Water Company at Campden Hill.

also built mansions, suburban churches at Highgate, Sydenham and Clapham, and the Law Society headquarters in Chancery Lane.

Water Tower

The "not inelegant" water tower which dominated Campden Hill from 1858 until its demolition in 1970 was complemented by covered reservoirs (1845 and 1868-9) and a pumping-station, all belonging to the Grand Junction Water Works Company. The tower inspired G K Chesterton's (*qv*) first novel.

George Frederic Watts

Entirely self-educated, Watts (1817-1904) benefited from the patronage of the Ionides family (*qv*) who commissioned many portraits from him, and from an introduction to Lord Holland when he was British minister in Florence. Holland made Watts his house guest for four years, enabling him to practise portraiture, fresco painting and modelling. Returning to London, Watts painted allegorical subjects for Dorchester House, Park Lane, which had been designed by Lewis Vulliamy (*qv*), and decorated ceilings at Holland House (*qv*). Taken up by the Prinsep family, he lived with them in Little Holland House for the next twenty-five years. Cursed by poor health, Watts was able, thanks to their protection, to live reclusively and ascetically and work industriously. The actress Ellen Terry was, briefly (1864-5) and disastrously, Watts's wife. Their marriage was probably never consummated and after Watts tired of using her as a model he arranged a legal separation but refused a divorce for over twenty years until he wanted to remarry. Despite his retiring nature, honours pursued him. In 1867 Watts was elected RA without his knowledge and in 1882 received honorary degrees from both Oxford and Cambridge. Faced with the prospect of leaving Little Holland House when the Prinseps' lease expired 'England's Michelangelo' built a house for them (and him occasionally) in the Isle of Wight, adjacent to Tennyson's and for himself a new 'Little Holland House' at 6 Melbury Road, where he lived from 1876 until his death. The architect was Frederick Pepys Cockerell,

138. *George Frederick Watts, known to friends and admirers as 'Signor', from a photograph by Ernest Mills.*

139. *Sir Aston Webb, a drawing by Fred Roe.*

Tytler (1850-1938), who looked after him devotedly. Watts died as a result of chill caught while working in the garden studio at Melbury Road. He left over 800 paintings. Half a dozen biographies and memoirs of Watts appeared within less than a decade, including one by G K Chesterton *(qv)*. Watts' house was demolished *c*.1965 to make way for Kingfisher House.[78]

Sir Aston Webb (1849-1930)

The architect who gave Buckingham Palace its current face lived at No. 1 Lansdowne Walk from 1890 until his death, remodelling the house to create in Pevsner's words "a picturesque composition of steep roofs and banded chimneys (not at all in the spirit of his classical public buildings)." Webb's major projects in Kensington included the main block of the Victoria and Albert Museum, the Royal College of Science, Royal School of Mines and Imperial College of Science and Technology. He was also

son of Charles Robert Cockerell. Cockerell provided three studios on the ground floor, two of which rose through the first floor. Val Prinsep gave up part of his garden so that Watts could enjoy larger 'grounds. (In 1881 Watts added an exhibition studio, open to the public on weekend afternoons). Watts now became interested in the work of the School of Needlework and the Arts and Crafts Guild. During this

period he also completed his most impressive statue, the colossal equestrian figure he called *Physical Energy*, which now stands in Kensington Gardens. A cast was taken to Cape Town as a memorial to Cecil Rhodes, whose career fascinated Watts and whose portrait he had painted. Watts twice declined the baronetcy offered by Gladstone but in 1886 found late happiness in his marriage to his wealthy Scottish pupil Mary Fraser responsible for the Admiralty Arch and the architectural setting of the Victoria Memorial. Further afield his works included Birmingham's law courts and university, Christ's Hospital School at Horsham and the Naval College at Dartford. Webb's excellence in planning, construction and ornamentation was abundantly recognised, both professionally and publicly. He served as President of the Royal Institute of British Architects, received its Royal Gold Medal, was knighted and in 1919 became only the second architect in its history to serve as President of the Royal Academy.

Chaim Weizmann (1874-1952)

The future first President of Israel moved into No. 67 Addison Road in 1917, the year of the Balfour Declaration, which was in part an acknowledgment of the crucial contribution Weizmann's expertise as a biochemist had made to Britain's explosives industry at a moment of military crisis. (On which see Lionel Davidson's ingenious thriller *The Sun Chemist*). Weizmann moved on in 1920 on becoming president of the World Zionist Organization.

N H J Westlake

In 1861 Westlake (1833-1921), who specialised in ecclesiastical paintings and stained-glass was living at 8 Gloucester Terrace, Clarendon Road, Notting Hill and working on paintings for the Roman Catholic church of St Francis *(qv)* in collaboration with the

140. *Chaim Weizmann.*

youthful J F Bentley. In 1863 Westlake commissioned Bentley's "first essay in purely domestic architecture", No. 235 Lancaster Road, at the corner with Treadgold Street. Westlake and Bentley were to collaborate on many other ecclesiastical projects.

Westway

Site clearance for this two mile long raised motorway began in 1964, construction in 1966. Even before it was completed Westway featured as the location of the fashion shoot in Michael Powell's *(qv)* 1968 film *Sebastian*. Construction involved the demolition of some 700 homes, including 10 Rillington Place, once occupied by the multiple

141. *Westway and Portobello Green market.*

murderer John Christie *(qv)*. Opened against a background of vocal local hostility by Minister of Transport Michael Heseltine in 1970, Westway was soon being used by 47,000 vehicles daily. Quotidien use did nothing to diminish its iconic power. In 1973 it supplied the setting for J G Ballard's *Concrete Island*, in which a driver crashes his car in the middle of the road but is unable to flag down any help from passing vehicles. In 1977 The Clash were photographed underneath the Westway as a back shot for their forthcoming album *The Clash*. In the same year The Jam used the same setting for the cover of their second album appropriately entitled *This Is The Modern World*.

Whiteley's

Whiteley's main premises did not move to Queensway until 1911 and originally stood on Westbourne Grove, where William Whiteley (1831-1907) had opened his first shop in 1863 with ten years' savings – £700. By 1867 he had premises on both sides of the street. By 1876 he had fifteen shops and 2,000 staff. The 'Universal Provider' diversified from drapery into dry goods, dry cleaning, estate agency and whatever else might endear him to the local bourgeoisie. The relentless expansion of Whiteley's establishment provoked the small traders of the locality into burning him in effigy in 1876. Various of his premises were destroyed by fire, quite possibly arson, on six occa-

sions, causing losses of £870,000. Whiteley just held massive salvage sales and bounced back. His own demise was as sudden as it was unexpected. In 1907 Horace George Rayner, claiming to be Whiteley's illegitimate son, shot him dead in his office when he refused to help him out of debt and then shot himself in the head. Rayner recovered to stand trial and, thanks to widespread public sympathy, was spared the rope. Whiteley's murder inspired the plotline of Julian Fellowes' Oscar-winning script for *Gosford Park*.

Whiteley's, which had become a limited company in 1899, moved into its imposing Queensway store, designed by Belcher and Joass, in 1911 but was taken over by

Gordon Selfridge in 1927. The store closed in 1981 and reopened as a shopping centre in 1989.[79]

World War One

Large numbers of local men served with the Royal Fusiliers, usually in the 13th Battalion ('Princess Louise's') or the 22nd ('The Kensingtons'). A superb collective portrait of men of the latter unit, exhausted by days of winter fighting – 'The Kensingtons at Laventie' – was painted by Eric Kennington and can be seen in the Imperial War Museum. The Museum also houses 'Old Bill', a bus from Middle Row Bus Garage, one of dozens famously used to rush British reinforcements to the front to contain the German offensive in the opening phase of the war. Dennis Brothers, coach-builders of Silchester Road, manufactured horse-drawn ambulances. Queen Elizabeth College (*qv*) opened a communal kitchen.

World War Two

Evacuation dispersed local children widely from Lancashire to the West Country. Anticipating gas raids, a decontamination plant was established at the Refuse Wharf on the Grand Junction Canal. Wornington Road School was taken over by the Auxiliary Fire Service. The Sunbeam Talbot factory in Barlby Road repaired Spitfire engines, Munro Engineering made parts for tanks and Globe-Wernicke switched down-market from turning out glass-fronted bookcases to ammunition boxes. What was claimed to be Britain's first 'British Restaurant' was opened in Dalgarno Gardens.

Michael X

Born Michael de Freitas (1933-75) in Trinidad, he was the son of an absentee Portuguese father. His mother was a local voodoo practitioner. De Freitas became a merchant seaman for a decade before becoming an enforcer for slum landlord Peter Rachman (*qv*). Variously described as a bully, a coward and a fraud, de Freitas discovered LSD and literature and in 1965 was dubbed Michael X by the *Sunday Times* as though he was a British equivalent of the charismatic American Black Power leader Malcolm X. De Freitas accepted the mantle and funds for various nominal and chaotic campaigning organisations. In his supposed capacity as a significant community leader he was introduced to such celebrities as Muhammad Ali, Dr Martin Luther King Jr., Sammy Davis Junior and John Lennon. As fashions changed in radical chic Michael X also became known as Michael Abdul Malik. Colin MacInnes (*qv*) liked de Freitas and William Burroughs declared him "a writer of considerable distinction". De Freitas achieved the dubious 'distinction' of being the first person to be arrested under Britain's newly-enacted Race Relations Act and served nine months in prison for an anti-white diatribe. After a period of involvement in social and cultural projects to better the condition of black people in Britain and making trips to Africa and Asia to meet Third World leaders, de Freitas found himself facing further legal charges and fled to Trinidad to live on a smallholding with his family and a few acolytes. Here he allowed the English girlfriend of a visiting American Black Muslim to become a human sacrifice and himself murdered a Trinidadian follower with a cutlass for disobedience. Fleeing to the Guyanese jungle, de Freitas was arrested and after 32 months on Death Row was hanged in his native Trinidad.[80]

Chronology

1591 Sir Walter Cope acquires West Town
1599 Sir Walter cope acquires the manor of St Mary Abbots
1612 Cope's Castle (Holland House) built
1683-1704 St Mary Abbots rebuilt
1698 Wells (Aubrey) House built
1711-12 Charity School built to the designs of Nicholas Hawksmoor
1714 Uxbridge Road turnpike trust established
1739 Admiral Vernon captures Puerto Bello
1766 Joshua Rhodes *Topographical Survey of the Parish of Kensington*
1801 Grand Junction (now Grand Union) Canal opened
1812 Dutch Garden and Irish Garden laid out at Holland House
1818 Pig-keeping colony established in Notting Dale by Samuel Lake
1820 Thomas Faulkner – *The History and Antiquities of Kensington*
1821-3 Ladbroke estate layout planned by Thomas Allason
1824 Bethesda chapel, Kensington Place opened
1827 Campden Hill Square begun
1829 St Barnabas, Addison Road completed
1831-2 Cholera epidemic
1833 Kensal Green cemetery consecrated
1837 Hippodrome opened
     Norland Square and Royal Crescent laid out
1838 Local section of the Great Western Railway built
1842 Hippodrome closed
     John Sinclair becomes vicar of St Mary Abbots
1843 Burial of the Duke of Sussex at Kensal Green Cemetery
1844 St John the Evangelist, Ladbroke Grove built
1845 St James Norlands consecrated
1846 Horbury Congregational Chapel (Kensington Temple) built
1849 Cholera outbreak
1850 Sun in Splendour public house built
     Ragged School opened in Kensal New Town
1854 Cholera outbreak
1857 St Peter's consecrated
     St Mary of the Angels consecrated

1852 St Peter, Kensington Park Road completed
1853-5 *Kensington Gazette* published
1858 Wesleyan chapel, Westbourne Grove completed
     Aubrey Walk pumping station built for Grand Union Junction Water Co.
     St Mary's RC cemetery opened
     Norland and Potteries Ragged School opened by Lord Shaftesbury
1860 St Francis, Pottery Lane completed
1861 All Saints' church, Talbot Road dedicated
1862 Franciscan Convent opened
1863 Bijou Theatre opened
     Cardinal Manning founds St Charles College
1864 Ladbroke Grove (then Notting Hill) station opened
     St George's church built
1865 Church of St Andrew destroyed by fire
1865-9 *Kensington and Chelsea News* published
1855 Leighton House designed
1869 St Clement, Treadgold Street, Notting Dale completed
     Kensington News and West London Times begins publication
1870 Queen's Park Estate developed by the Artisans' Labourers' and General Dwellings Company
1871 St Michael Ladbroke Grove completed
1872 Reconstruction of St Mary Abbots completed
1873 Edenham Street crèche started
1874 Prince of Wales public house opened
     James Heywood's library opened at 106 Notting Hill Gate
     Wornington Road School built
1878 Middle Row school opened
1879 Notting Hill Methodist church built on the site of the former St Andrew's
     Colville School, Lonsdale Road opened
1881 St Charles Hospital, Barlby Road completed
1882 Our Lady of the Holy Souls, Bosworth Road, Kensal Town completed
     Cobden Working Men's Club and Institute opened in Kensal Road

1883	Observatory Gardens built	1953	Execution of John Christie
1884	St Helen, St Helen's Gardens completed		Kensington Society formed
1887	Talbot Tabernacle, Talbot Road opened	1955	Pushkin Club founded

1883 Observatory Gardens built
1884 St Helen, St Helen's Gardens completed
1887 Talbot Tabernacle, Talbot Road opened
1888 Lancaster Road Baths and Wash House opened
     Silchester Road baths completed
1889 Rugby Boys' Club founded in Walmer Road
     St John the Baptist, Holland Road completed
     St Thomas, Kensal Road completed
1892 Avondale Park opened
1893 Our Lady of Sion convent completed
1894 Public Library, Ladbroke Grove completed
     Faraday Road fire station opened
1895 General Omnibus Company stables opened in Conlan Street
1898 Coronet Theatre built
     Campden Hill Court built
1899 London Government Act divides Kensal area between Kensington and Paddington
1900 Notting Hill Synagogue opened
     Holland Park station opened
     Improved Tenements Association founded
     Lansdowne House built
1901 Anglican church of St Columb, Lancaster Road opened
1904 Publication of G K Chesterton's *The Napoleon of Notting Hill*
1910 Electric Palace cinema built
     Byam Shaw School of Drawing and Painting opened
1915 Queen Elizabeth College campus established on Campden Hill
1920 Rowe Housing Trust established
1924 Kensington Housing Trust established
1928 Spanish and Portuguese Synagogue, St James's Gardens opened
1931 Mercury Theatre established
1936 Wornington Road school demolished and rebuilt
1939 Geales restaurant opened
     West London Crematorium opened
1941 Destruction of Holland House
1948 Temporary closure of the Caledonian market stimulates antique trade on Portobello Road
1949 Campden Hill Preservation Society formed
1951 Church of St Columb sold to Serbian community
1952 London County Council takes over Holland Park

1953 Execution of John Christie
     Kensington Society formed
1955 Pushkin Club founded
     Moray Lodge demolished
1955-7 Demolition of Holland House – Youth Hostel built
1957 Rent Act passed
1958 Notting Hill 'race riots'
     Holland Park School completed
1959 Our Lady of Mount Carmel, Kensington Church Street completed
     Sir Oswald Mosley defeated in parliamentary election for North Kensington
     Murder of Kelso Cochrane
1960 Central Library, Phillimore Walk completed
     Britain's first Adventure Playground opens in Golborne
1962 Formation of the Notting Hill Social Council
     Commonwealth Institute completed
1963 Notting Hill Housing Trust established
     Cardinal Vaughan RC school, Addison Road completed
1964 First Notting Hill carnival begins as a children's street party
1965 North West London Press acquires the *Kensington News*
1968 *Performance* starring Mick Jagger and James Fox filmed in Powis Square
1969 Notting Hill Books opened
     Kensal New Town Estate opened
1970 Westway opened
     Jimi Hendrix takes a fatal overdose at the Samarkand Hotel, Lansdowne Crescent
     North Kensington Law Centre opened
     Western Gas Works ceases production
1971 North Kensington Community Trust established
1972 Trellick Tower completed
1974 Murder of James Pope-Hennessey
1975 Demolition of Lancaster Road Baths and Wash House
1976 Riots at Notting Hill Carnival
     Completion of Civic Centre, Phillimore Walk
1977 'Free and Independent Republic of Frestonia' declared
1979 Gate Theatre established
     Travel Bookshop opened
1981 Pepper Pot Lunch Club for Caribbean seniors opened
1983 Books for Cooks opened
     Union of parishes of St Peter's and St John's
     Lisboa Patisserie opened

1984	Trellick Tower Residents' Association formed
1985	Union of parishes of St James and St Clement's
1986	London Lighthouse opened
	St Peter's Kensington Park road reopened
1987	Mercury Theatre converted
	Moroccan Information and Advice Centre opened
1988	Kensington Park road Cabbies' Shelter restored
	Statue of St Volodymyr erected
1991	Petersberg Press closed
1992	'Turquoise Island' public convenience opened by Lucinda Lambton
	Notting Hill Improvements Group established
1993	Kensington and Chelsea College established
1994	Somali Supplementary School opened
1996	Garden Books opened
	Murder of Ossie Clark
	Portobello Film Festival begins
1998	Phamarcy Bar and Restaurant opened
1999	Film *Notting Hill* released
	The Churchill Arms becomes *Evening Standard* Pub of the Year
2000	Closure of Notting Hill Synagogue
2001	Electric Cinema reopened
	Prince of Wales opened Al-Manaar Muslim Cultural and Heritage Centre

142. *The cabbies' shelter in Kensington Park Road*

143. *Kensal House, designed by Maxwell Fry (see p38).*

Footnotes

1   Alan Shestack, *Edwin Austin Abbey,* Yale UP, 1973

2   Diana Brooks, *Thomas Allom,* Heinz Gallery/RIBA, 1998

3   Mary Stocks, *My Commonplace Book,* 1970; *Still More Commonplace,*1973

4   www.mysite.freeserve.com/wgc

5   www.bennbiography.com

6   www.booksforcooks.com

7   www.netreach.net/~druid/FB/;www.musicweb.uk.net/bridge/

8   J M Crook, *William Burges and the High Victorian Dream,*1981

9   www.billbrandt.com

10   www.byam-shaw.ac.uk

11   www.campdencharities.org.uk

12   www.churcharmy.org

13   www.buildingsoflondon.co.uk/pm/carnival

14   www.sirhughcasson.com; Jose Manser *Hugh Casson: A Biography,* 2000

15   www.gilbertmagazine.com;www.chesterston.org;www.dur.ac.uk/martin.ward/gkc/

16   www.parmaq.com/truecrime/Rillington.htm

17   Antony Blight, *Georges Roesch and the Invincible Talbot,* 1970

18   Jan O'Malley, *The politics of community action: a decade of struggle in Notting Hill,* Bertrand Russell Peace Foundation for Spokesman Books

19   www.garwayroadmedicalcentre.co.uk/

20   www.sirwilliamrussellflint.com

21   Max Saunders *Ford Madox Ford: A Dual Life: The After-War World* Oxford UP, 1996; Douglas Goldring *South Lodge: reminiscences of Violet Hunt, Ford Madox Ford and the English Review circle,* Folcroft 1977; www.rialto.com/fordmadoxford_society/

22   www.globalideasbank.org/Frestonia.html

23   Maxwell Fry, *Autobiographical Sketches,* Elek 1975

24   http://math.boisestate.edu/gas/

25   Ruth Dudley Edwards *Victor Gollancz: A Biography,* 1987

26   www.canalmuseum.org.uk

27   www.hardysociety.org;www.yale.edu/hardysoc/

28   Peter Schlesinger, *A Chequered Past – My Visual Diary of the 60s and 70s,* Thames and Hudson 2004

29   www.hollandpark.kensington-chelsea.sch.uk

30   www.bodley.ox.ac.uk/dept/scwmss

31   www.kcchg.org.uk; www.golbornehistory.org.uk

32   Kwesi Bacchra, *Claudia Jones: A Life in Exile,* 2000

33   H Vivian-Neal (ed.) *Paths of Glory,* Friends of Kensal Green Cemetery 1997 www.kensalgreen.co.uk; www.kensalgreen.net

34   Jerome Borkwood, *From Kensal Village to Golborne Road – Tales of the Inner City,* Kensington & Chelsea Community History Group 2003 www.golbornehistory.org

35   www.elim.org.uk

36   www.ladbrokeassociation.btinternet.co.uk

37   www.cts-lansdowne.co.uk/

38   www.laosheteahouse.com/en/

39   Recent studies include those of Christopher Newall (1990), Russell Ash (1995), an RA catalogue of 1996 and Tim Barringer and Elizabeth Prettejohn (eds.) *Frederic Leighton: Antiquity, Renaissance, Modernity* (1999).

40   www.rbkc.gov.uk/LHLeightonHouse

41   www.futurism.org.uk/

42   www.rbkc.gov.uk/libraries/
43   David Linnell, *Blake, Palmer, Linnell & Co.* Book Guild, 1994; A T Story's 1892 biography of Linnell
     is accessible online at www.victorianweb.org/painting/linnell/story/conyents.html. His archive is at
     the Fitzwilliam Museum www.fitzmuseum.cam.ac.uk/msspb/exhibit/Linnell/
44   www.machensoc.demon.co.uk
45   www.lib.rochester.edu/rbk/MACINNES.stm; Tony Gould *Inside Outsider: The Life and Times of Colin
     MacInnes,* Hogarth Press 1983
46   Lytton Strachey's sceptical sketch of Manning's life in *Eminent Victorians* is well worth reading.
47   www.rylibweb.man.ac.uk/data2/spcoll/eicp/
48   *The Street Photographs of Roger Mayne,* Zelda Cheatle Press 1993
     Roger Mayne, *Photographs,* Jonathan Cape 2001
49   *James McBey: A Portrait of the Artist,* Boston Public Library 1985
     James McBey The Early Life of James McBey, Canongate 1993
50   www.stellamccartney.com
51   www.mediterraneangardensociety.org/people/Archibald.Menzies.html
52   www. montessori.ac.uk
53   Nicholas Mosley *Rules of the Game, Beyond the Pale,* Pimlico 1998; www.oswaldmosley.com
54   Jane E Sayers, *The fountain unsealed: a history of the Notting Hill and Ealing High School,* 1973
55   Bernard Crick, *George Orwell* www.k-1.com/Orwell/
56   www.pembridgeassociation.org.uk
57   J G Paul Delaney, *Glyn Philpot: His Life and Art,* 1999
58   www.portobelloroad.co.uk
59   www.powell-pressburger.org
60   Una Troubridge published *The Life of Radclyffe Hall* in 1961. Sally Cline, *Radclyffe Hall: A Woman
     Called John,* 1997; Diana Souhami, *The Trials of Radclyffe Hall* 1998
61   www.rambert.org.uk
62   www.redonda.org
63   *The Art of Zandra Rhodes,* Jonathan Cape 1984; www.zandrarhodes.com
64   Edward Pilkington, *Beyond the Mother Country: West Indians and the Notting Hill White Riots*
     I.B. Tauris & Co. 1990.
65   www.stgeorgescampdenhill.com
66   www.w11opera.org
67   Past worshippers included Isaac Newton, Joseph Addison, Thomas Hardy *(qqv),* William Wilberforce
     and Beatrix Potter. Whistler, Kipling, Pound *(qv)* and Chesterton *(qv)* were all married here.
     www.stmaryabbotschurch.org
68   www.rbkc.gov.uk/linleysambournehouse
69   David L. Chapman, *Sandow the Magnificent: Eugene Sandow and the Beginnings of Bodybuilding,* 1994
     www.sandowplus.com
70   www.sassoonery.demon.co.uk
71   www.cyburbia.net/Community/mcdsss/
72   www.tabernacle.org.uk
73   www.thetravelbookshop.co.uk
74   Nigel Warburton, *Erno Goldfinger: The Life of an Architect,* Routledge 2003
75   www.victorianturkishbath.org
76   www.evelynunderhill.org
77   www.virgin.com
78   www.wattsgallery.org; W Blunt, England's Michelangelo, 1975.
79   Erika Diane Rappaport, *Shopping for Pleasure: Women in the Making of London's West End,* Princeton
     UP 2000; www.whiteleys.com

Index

An asterisk denotes an illustration or caption.